Career Paths in
the Field of Aging

Career Paths in the Field of Aging

Professional Gerontology

David A. Peterson
Ethel Percy Andrus Gerontology Center
University of Southern California

Lexington Books
D.C. Heath and Company/Lexington, Massachusetts/Toronto

Library of Congress Cataloging-in-Publication Data

Peterson, David A. (David Alan), 1937–
  Career paths in the field of aging.

  Includes index.
  1. Gerontology—Vocational guidance—United States.
I. Title. [DNLM: 1. Geriatrics. WT 21 P485c]
HQ1064.U5P468   1987   362.6'042'02373   86–46269
ISBN 0–669–15282–X (alk. paper)
ISBN 0–669–15283–8 (pbk. : alk. paper)

Published simultaneously in Canada
Printed in the United States of America
Casebound International Standard Book Number: 0–669–15282–X
Paperbound International Standard Book Number: 0–669–15283–8
Library of Congress Catalog Card Number 86–46269

The paper used in this publication meets the minimum requirements of
American National Standard for Information Sciences—Permanence of
Paper for Printed Library Materials, ANSI Z 39.48–1984. ∞™

87 88 89 90 91 8 7 6 5 4 3 2

Contents

Figure and Tables

Figure

Tables

Purpose of the Book

This book focuses on professionals in the field of gerontology and on the services for older people that are now being developed and delivered by a large number of practitioners, some who call themselves gerontologists and some who see themselves as working within another profession. The book does not deal with older people or growing old per se. Nor does it deal primarily with the social issues faced by the poor, the handicapped, the disenfranchised elderly, or minority group members. Rather, it emphasizes the preparation, occupations, activities, and employment of personnel who work with and for older people. Thus, the issues to be dealt with are those of professionals.

This book explores the current state of gerontology employment and how it got that way; the trends that are evident; and the goals toward which gerontology professionals are moving. It will help students to begin to formulate answers to such basic questions as:

Who are gerontologists?

What do gerontologists do?

Where do gerontologists work?

How do gerontologists differ from persons in other professions?

Is gerontology a good field to enter?

There are no universally accepted answers to these questions; the field is not fixed, stable, or stagnant. Much change still is under way, and final descriptions of the roles of professionals and the agencies in which they work are still in development.

This book will help current and future gerontology practitioners develop self-awareness; it analyzes what people in gerontology are doing now, what they will do in the future, how the field is viewed by others, and how graduates of instructional programs have fared. In helping to build the field, this book represents the first attempt to review the literature comprehensively in order to understand what has happened to this point and to identify some preferred directions for the future.

The long-term goal is to help potential professionals fit into this developing field. It is important for all professionals to gain an understanding of the field in which they may choose to work and to be able to assess its future viability. This orientation is not explored in any other gerontology book, hence the need and purpose for this book.

To describe the current status of gerontology professionals, however, the terms to be used must be clearly understood. Consistency will aid understanding, but it should be kept in mind that none of these terms is universally accepted. *Gerontology* is used to denote a field of study and practice. Emphasis in the past has been on the scientific knowledge that is available. Today, we need to include the activity of providing services and products to older people when using the term, and we must include the professional providers of such services and products when we describe gerontologists.

The term *field of aging* is used to refer to the planning, administration, and service delivery network that is designed primarily or exclusively for *older people,* generally considered to be those over sixty years of age. This network includes the Administration on Aging National Aging Network and much more: nursing homes, mental health and social services, housing, recreation, rehabilitation, education, transportation, nutrition, adult day care programs, chronic disease hospitals, and many other services and institutions. *Gerontology instruction* refers to preservice instruction and continuing education in gerontology. It includes a variety of instructional purposes and outcomes and is offered at all levels of higher education. Gerontology instruction is important primarily for occupational fields that students normally enter after a period of formal education, generally in a postsecondary educational institution. Our interests here are primarily with those job opportunities that include some preservice training, from at least a few weeks to as much as several years.

A *professional gerontologist* is a person who has completed an education to become a practitioner in the field of aging. Normally it is assumed that planning, administration, or service to older people constitutes a significant portion of the professional gerontologist's workload, say, at least one-half time. Finally, *gerontologist* is a broad term that includes everyone involved in the field of aging or in research and teaching about that field.

This book includes some material that has been written for other works. Parts of Chapter Five will be published in a forthcoming issue of *Educational Gerontology;* a portion of Chapter Six was published in the spring 1985 issue of *Gerontology and Geriatrics Education;* and some of Chapter Seven was published in the October 1985 issue of *The Gerontologist.*

I would like to express my appreciation to David Bergstone, Donna

Deutchman, and May Ng who assisted with the data analysis, editing, and word processing, and to the staff of the Leonard Davis School of Gerontology who provided encouragement and advice throughout the writing process.

Career Paths in
the Field of Aging

1
Introduction to Gerontology as a Disciplinary Field

Gerontology is typically defined as the study of the processes of aging, those multiple and interrelated changes that affect the biological, behavioral, and social aspects of our lives. The results of these processes become more pronounced over time and by the later stages of life are such that older people are frequently seen as different from middle-aged and younger individuals. An inverted U curve is generally used to describe the growth, stability and senescence of the body's systems, and it frequently is used by analogy to describe the mental and social life stages of the individual. Aging is sometimes confused with illness, although recent scientific studies have made progress toward describing "normal" aging and toward distinguishing it from age-related disease, as well as identifying the areas where individual or societal change can enhance life's quality and extend its length.

Gerontology, then, is multidisciplinary, drawing upon the best science from a number of fields, each with its own body of knowledge, methods of research, and organized groups to disseminate new information. As aging has been studied with greater intensity and sophistication, understanding of its processes has increased. Although it is not yet possible to predict how rapidly any individual will age or what the specific accompaniments will be for each person, much progress has been made in understanding the general attributes of the processes of aging.

Although typically defined in the above manner, gerontology is more than just the *study* of the processes of aging. It also includes providing service to older people and to their families; this is the *practice* of gerontology. This field of practice includes many professionals and paraprofessionals whose primary purpose, in contrast to learning more about the processes of aging, is oriented toward applying what is known in relevant and helpful ways to alleviate some of the problems that frequently accompany old age, prevent others, and enhance the opportunities for personal growth. One example of these professional roles is that of the counselor who works on a one-to-one basis with an older person to help him or her adjust to the loss of a spouse, to seek a new job, to acquire the government benefits that are legally due, or to plan for a secure financial future. Another example is the program planner who secures funding for a new service; who plans and organizes the staff and physical facility; who supervises group programs in recreation, education, travel, or support systems; and/or who evaluates the program and seeks refinements that will improve and stabilize it in the future. Perhaps the most common example is the administrator who oversees ongoing programs of an institution or agency, balances the budget, supervises personnel, seeks innovation and growth, maintains the physical facility, and deals with the myriad details involved in the delivery of human services.

Gerontology professionals carry out a variety of roles in as many service areas as older persons have needs, for instance in health, social services, education, recreation, housing, transportation, information and referral, income maintenance, job placement, mental health, and rehabilitation. The roles and the service areas are so new that they are still developing and are so diverse that it is difficult to be very precise in describing exactly what a "practicing" gerontologist does.

Gerontology, then, has two orientations: first, that of a *discipline* devoted to study of the processes of aging, a philosophical or scientific approach focused on the acquisition of new knowledge or greater insight into the meaning of aging; and second, that of a field of *practice* in which professionals and paraprofessionals plan, provide, and administer a variety of services to aging individuals.

Gerontology as a Discipline

The field of gerontology is often described in several different ways: as a discipline, as a multidisciplinary field of study, or as a profession. Each of these terms reflects a part of the history and present composition of the field. Closer examination is needed to understand the meaning of these concepts and to suggest the implications that result from the choice of any one of them.

As has been noted, gerontology is frequently described as a *discipline,* an organized body of knowledge and a means of finding and replicating that knowledge (methods of research). The goal of a discipline is truth, where truth is defined as facts, typically as empirical knowledge that can describe, predict, and ultimately control certain processes, in this case aging.

The orientation is to knowledge, the organization of knowledge, and scientific inquiry that will lead to knowing and understanding. In this view, knowledge need not be directly useful in order to have value; it has intrinsic value and is sought for its own sake. Thus, researchers are often referred to as being in an "ivory tower," separate from the rest of society, because they are seeking knowledge without any particular concern for the relevance of this knowledge to the contemporary social situation. A term of derision, it is taken by many in higher education as a compliment. In their view, scientists should seek truth, rather than worry about the problems of the community.

A discipline is frequently defined as meeting the following criteria:

1. It has a general body of knowledge that can be forced into some reasonably logical taxonomy

2. It has a specialized vocabulary and a generally accepted basic literature

3. It has a generally accepted body of theory and some generally understood techniques for theory testing and revision

4. It has a generally agreed-upon methodology

5. It has a set of recognized techniques for replication and revalidation of research and scholarship (Dressel and Mayhew 1974)

The question must then be asked, is gerontology a discipline? Most scientific gerontologists work within the traditional disciplines of biology, psychology, sociology, political science, economics, literature, history, and religion. Also, most seem to agree that gerontology is not a separate discipline but an adjunct or specialization within one or several of these existing fields. Further, they agree that gerontology is not likely to become a discipline in the near future (see Loeb 1979; Johnson 1980; Peterson and Bolton 1980; Levine 1981). In contrast, Bramwell (1985) has made a recent argument that gerontology *should* be considered as a discipline, and Seltzer (1985) concluded that if gerontology is not already an academic discipline, it is rapidly becoming one because it not only draws on other disciplines but has developed some concepts, perspectives, knowledge, and methods that are uniquely its own. However, although gerontology does have a body of knowledge and some basic literature, at this time it does not appear to have a body of theory, a special methodology, or specific replication approches. Rather, scientific gerontology relies on the methods of other disciplines to generate and replicate knowledge about aging and older people. Thus, it does not at present meet the criteria of a discipline.

This does not mean that gerontology will never become a discipline. Persistent attempts are being made to develop gerontological theory, such as that by the Institute for Advanced Study of the Andrus Gerontology Center, University of Southern California, and some new methodological approaches are being developed, such as Schaie's cross-sequential analysis (Schaie and Hertzog 1985). Still, it appears that gerontology is not yet a discipline, despite the relatively modest efforts to generate approaches and arguments for it to become one. For this reason, most scientific gerontology faculty prefer to see research on aging conducted within the confines of one or more of those disciplines that are currently in place.

Another approach is to consider gerontology a *multidiscipline,* a field that draws on other existing disciplines and professions. A multidiscipline thus defined is a cooperative effort involving people and knowledge from a variety of disciplines for the purpose of accomplishing coordinated and complementary objectives. Frequently, it involves no real integration, just a common interest (aging) viewed from several different fields. The task of a multidiscipline is to develop:

1. An organizational setting in which more than one discipline or profession is represented
2. Research tools composed of skills, methods, and concepts from different disciplines or professions
3. The organizational and professional capacity to operate successfully in such settings, actually using knowledge from different disciplines and professions in adequately solving tasks (Salmon-Cox and Hozner 1977)

Multidisciplinary groups can take on different appearances depending upon whether they are oriented to research, service, or education, and whether they involve disciplines or professions. Gerontology incorporates a number of multidisciplinary efforts. From a professional point of view, multi-disciplinary team approaches to providing physical health, mental health, or social services are now becoming more evident. The team is a functioning unit composed of individuals with varied and specialized training who coordinate their activities to provide the services to a client or group of clients (Ducanis and Golin 1979). By sharing insights from several professionals, the team can more completely understand and address the multiple and inter-related problems facing the older person.

Likewise, multidisciplinary approaches to research are also increasingly evident in gerontology. They are used to bring together persons from several disciplines in order to apply insights from each to unraveling the processes of aging. Much has yet to be learned about how to integrate the differing methodological approaches effectively, but realization of the value of this integration is widespread, and its use is increasing.

Gerontology service and research today seem to have gone beyond a multidisciplinary approach and are in the process of creating new institutions, new programs, and new instruction totally oriented to older people. Although the criteria for a multidisciplinary field are much less precise than are those for a discipline, it seems reasonable to conclude that gerontology has more than met the criteria for a multidisciplinary field and needs to be seen as something more.

A Brief History of Disciplinary Gerontology

The disciplinary perspective is composed of two parts: liberal arts and scientific investigation. To understand better the multiple aspects of the field of gerontology, we will look briefly at the history of its development to examine why the field is so diverse and why it sometimes appears to be moving in several directions simultaneously.

Liberal Gerontology. This approach to gerontology is not recognized widely, although it is the oldest and has dominated thinking on the subject for centuries. It has been called an interest in liberal gerontology, a parallel to the study of liberal arts, and its purpose is to acquire a philosophical understanding and appreciation of the processes of aging. The liberal arts are aimed at liberating the individual from the bonds of ignorance, prejudice, and cultural isolation. They emphasize meaning, and in the case of gerontology, the meaning of life and the meaning of age. Liberal gerontology is found in philosophical and religious orientations and is most commonly approached through the humanities and arts, for instance, through literature, poetry, history, art, drama, dance, and other forms of cultural expression.

Liberal gerontology has ancient roots. The early Greeks and Egyptians were concerned with aging, as well as with the afterlife. Their interest was not scientific as we know it today, but speculative and based on conjecture. It was used to explore and contemplate the meaning of aging and its value to society. Shakespeare discussed the seven ages of man. The Spanish sought the fountain of youth in the New World. There has always been a strong interest in aging and its meaning, its value, and the value of older people.

This orientation emphasizes breadth of knowledge, integration of the knowledge into a whole, and theory building that will answer the larger philosophical questions of life. It focuses on personal development, aiding the individual to grow and to make the best use of the personal capabilities. For instance, gerontologists with this orientation have examined the attitudes toward and conditions of older people in various historical periods. They have also used philosophical approaches to examine the attitudes toward aging and have sought to discover the ways in which aging is portrayed in various types of literature and media.

Although this approach was the earliest to develop, it has not gained extensive visibility or popularity within gerontology. This lack has occurred partly because of the decline in interest in the humanities, and partly because of our current preference for data-based explanations rather than philosophical ones. However, a small but growing number of faculty members in colleges and universities have taken this orientation, and there is an expanding awareness of the value that this approach can bring. More liberal gerontology courses are now being offered, frequently including material that deals with the meaning of aging, attitudes toward aging and older people, wisdom, and an understanding of the significance of aging for the individual and society.

Scientific Gerontology. The second orientation is frequently referred to as scientific or empirical gerontology. This orientation's purpose is to describe, predict, and ultimately control aging. Aging is considered a fascinating intellectual problem. Questions addressed include: Why does aging occur? What is normal and what is pathological? How long is the possible life span? What controls the processes of aging? How can aging be separated from cohort and accidental events? How does intellectual ability change with age? What impact does retirement have on life satisfaction? Do spirituality and religiosity change with age?

Distinctly scientific interest in aging has existed for approximately one hundred years, involving attempts to describe aging processes and ultimately gain some control over aspects of them. The earliest studies, undertaken in the late 1800s by biologists, included aging as one of many variables to be considered. Research was done on both plants and animals, and several books on aging were published during the first twenty years of this century (Birren 1961). Cowdry's works in the 1930s and 1940s moved interest into the medical area, and G. Stanley Hall's book *Senescence* (1922) opened the area of psychological study.

Organization building in gerontology began during this period. Stanford University established a research unit in psychological gerontology in the late 1920s, and interest in life span development grew rapidly. Longitudinal studies in Kansas City (by the University of Chicago) and at Duke University were conducted. Sociological studies, which did not begin until the 1940s, initially examined rural aging and old age in other cultures. The original handbooks on aging were published around 1960 and provided an impressive compilation of scientific data on aging from biological-psychological, anthropological, and sociological points of view (Birren 1959; Burgess 1960; Tibbitts 1960). Other publications followed in rapid succession as empirical research on aging gained increased attention.

As was noted earlier, throughout its history scientific inquiry has been based on the premise that knowledge has intrinsic value and that its verification and expansion are sufficient purposes for its pursuit. It emphasizes the importance of knowledge of previous findings; research methodology, using approved techniques and procedures to collect and analyze data; and verification through replication and open review. Studies generally concentrate on a small area that can be examined in depth, an area in which knowledge can be gained by building upon the findings of others. The purpose of scientific study is to obtain verified data, empirical findings that can be organized into theories that explain natural and social phenomena. The important outcome is knowledge that will lead toward a more complete explanation of the processes of aging and, in the very distant future, prediction or control of specific processes that are deleterious.

Scientific gerontology has expanded rapidly in the past few years, as concern about the implications of aging has increased. Most major universities now have basic and applied research units that focus specifically on aspects of aging, and government and foundation funding continues to grow. Although it does not appear that a breakthrough in understanding the aging processes is imminent, knowledge of all aspects of aging is rapidly accumulating, and the pace of knowledge acquisition should be rapid in the years ahead.

Conclusion

Gerontology as a discipline can be seen as having distinct historical roots that have developed into the liberal and scientific orientations of the field. These orientations derive from different interests and motivations and are manifested in different types of research, instruction, and service. As a different way of seeing the field of gerontology, each is valuable and valued because it facilitates important outcomes.

Another strain of historical development and view of the field is that of gerontology as a profession, the orientation emphasized in the remainder of this book. Although the need and value of scientific and liberal gerontology will remain evident, they are a secondary focus of this work, distinct from the primary emphasis, which is placed on the preparation and roles of professional staff who are employed in the planning, administration, and provision of services to older persons and their families.

References

Birren, J.E. (1961). A brief history of the psychology of aging. *The Gerontologist,* *1,* 67–77.

Birren, J.E. (Ed.) (1959). *Handbook of aging and the individual.* Chicago: University of Chicago Press.

Bramwell, R.D. (1985). Gerontology as a discipline. *Educational Gerontology, 11,* 201–210.

Burgess, E.W. (Ed.) (1960). *Aging in western societies: A survey of social gerontology.* Chicago: University of Chicago Press.

Cowdry, E.V. (Ed.) (1939). *Problems of aging.* Baltimore: Walhams and Wilkins.

Dressel, P.L., & Mayhew, L.B. (1974). *Higher education as a field of study.* San Francisco: Jossey-Bass.

Ducanis, A.J., & Golin, A.K. (1979). *The interdisciplinary health care team.* Germantown, Md.: Aspen Systems Corporation.

Hall, G.S. (1922). *Senescence, the second half of life.* New York: Appleton.

Johnson, H.R. (1980). Introduction. In C. Tibbitts, H. Friedsam, P. Kerschner, G. Maddox, & H. McClusky (Eds.), *Academic gerontology: Dilemmas of the 1980s.* Ann Arbor: University of Michigan Institute of Gerontology.

Levine, M. (1981). Guest editorial: Does gerontology exist? *The Gerontologist, 21,* 2–3.

Loeb, M.B. (1979). Gerontology is not a profession—the oldest or the youngest. In H.L. Sterns, E.F. Ansello, B.M. Sprouse, & R. Layfield-Faux (Eds.), *Gerontology in higher education: Developing institutional and community strength.* Belmont, Calif.: Wadsworth.

Peterson, D.A., & Bolton, C.R. (1980). *Gerontology instruction in higher education.* New York: Springer.

Salmon-Cox, L., & Hozner, B. (1977). *Managing multidisciplinarity: Building and bridging epistomologies in education, research, and development.* Paper presented at the AERA Learning Research and Development Center Meeting, University of Pittsburgh.

Schaie, K.W., & Hertzog, C. (1985). Measurement in the psychology of adulthood and aging. In J.E. Birren & K.W. Schaie (Eds.), *Handbook of the psychology of aging.* New York: Van Nostrand Reinhold.

Seltzer, M.M. (1985). Issues of accreditation of academic gerontology programs and credentialing of workers in the field of aging. *Gerontology and Geriatrics Education, 5,* 7–18.

Tibbitts, C. (Ed.) (1960). *Handbook of social gerontology.* Chicago: University of Chicago Press.

2
The Field of Gerontology as a Profession

The third gerontological orientation, professional practice, came about because of demographic changes in society and the social and personal problems that resulted. The growth of the older population has increased the visibility of age as an issue, and our collective concern for social justice has raised awareness of the vulnerability of many older people. The social needs of older people are rooted in many areas: housing, finances, health, mental health, adjustment, growth, transportation, friendships, and family relations, to name only a few.

Programs have been developed in these areas and in others to assist older individuals, both those who are frail and vulnerable and those who are seeking opportunities for growth and new challenges to pursue. An aging coalition has been developed that includes older people, bureaucrats, politicians, professionals, and academics who advocate on behalf of vulnerable older people, emphasizing their difficulties in order to secure greater resources and services. This coalition has been reasonably successful in securing government funding and in increasing the awareness of foundations, corporations, and philanthropists so that, more and more, funds are available from diverse sources to help older people.

Likewise, the growth of the older population and the recognition of its needs and wants has led to the realization that older persons are a desirable consumer group. Initially, most services and products were developed and provided by organizations and institutions that served all age groups, such as health care in hospitals, social services in welfare departments, leisure activities through parks and recreation programs, and so on. However, as recognition increased, age-segregated services and marketing strategies developed, targeting the older person as the primary or exclusive client. New products and services, including investment instruments, home health care products, travel opportunities, patent medicines, and health care facilities, are being marketed as both nonprofit and profit-making organizations attempt to determine and provide products that will be of interest to older consumers.

Products and services for older people require that well-prepared personnel be available to design, sell, and maintain them. In this regard, corporations do not need liberally educated gerontologists who understand history or philosophy, nor scientists who spend their time in the laboratory, but rather professionals who are knowledgeable about the needs and wants of older people, are concerned about the quality of later life, and have the skills necessary to design and provide the services and products.

The functions carried out by these professionals appear to fall into three general categories (Craig 1980). First, there are service programs providing direct assistance to older people and their families in the home, community, or institution. Second, there are administrative and planning functions that are carried out at the local, state, or federal levels of government or in voluntary agencies. Third, there are research and teaching activities that are undertaken by colleges and universities, nonprofit organizations, and for-profit research and evaluation firms.

It is surprising that so little attention has been paid in the literature to occupational roles in gerontology and, specifically, to the roles for professional gerontologists. This heretofore underanalyzed but rapidly growing field currently provides both outstanding opportunities for employment and intriguing questions regarding preparation, quality control, and future status.

Professions

Professions are different from disciplines in that their purpose is to solve social and community problems and to provide service. Professions, like disciplines, are based on knowledge. However, the aim of a profession is to *apply* knowledge, rather than to gain knowledge for its own sake. To the extent that gerontology is a profession, its emphasis is on social consciousness and a commitment to the applied.

In a sense, a profession seals a social bargain between its members and society. In return for special prerogatives and privileges, including social status, restrictions on entry and competition, and monetary rewards, the profession agrees to a certain measure of self-policing, supporting those structures and making them more effective. The literature on professions is voluminous, and although many different lists of characteristics can be found, the following attributes are typically included. A profession

1. Is a full-time occupation that provides a principal source of income to its practitioners
2. Typically involves a strong motivation or sense of calling and results in long-term dedication to the field and identification with it

3. Relates to a specialized body of knowledge and skills that are acquired during a prolonged period of education and training

4. Has a clear service orientation that requires the practitioner to use his or her expertise on behalf of the client

5. Involves autonomy of performance—that is, it is composed of professionals who are in a position to know what is best for the client because of their specialized knowledge

6. Generally forms professional organizations that establish and monitor standards of performance and admission to the profession, such as completion of an accredited training program and achieving licensed or certified status

7. Achieves a monopoly on the delivery of certain services that can only be performed by credentialed personnel

8. Has a code of ethics that provides guidance on the moral questions that confront professionals

Some occupational fields meet all these criteria and are appropriately considered to be full-fledged professions. Others meet some of the criteria but not all, and the question is then raised, are they professions? Aside from a few of the obvious examples—for instance, medicine and law—most occupational fields are not full professions but have many of the characteristics, and their practitioners want to continue the field's movement toward professionalization. Thus, it is too simplistic to categorize occupational fields only in dichotomous terms, either as professions or nonprofessions. More accurately, it is possible to place most occupations along a continuum between nonprofessions and full professions.

Carr-Saunders and Wilson (1964) have refined this approach by suggesting that professionalization is a dynamic process involving several stages of development; thus, one can speak of movement toward full professionalization. In the process of professionalization, an occupation changes its fundamental characteristics in order to become a profession—generally considered to be a positive value since it provides status, autonomy, and economic rewards. Most occupational groups would prefer to move in this direction.

The stages of professionalization include

1. Would-be professions
2. Semiprofessions
3. New professions
4. Established professions (see figure 2–1)

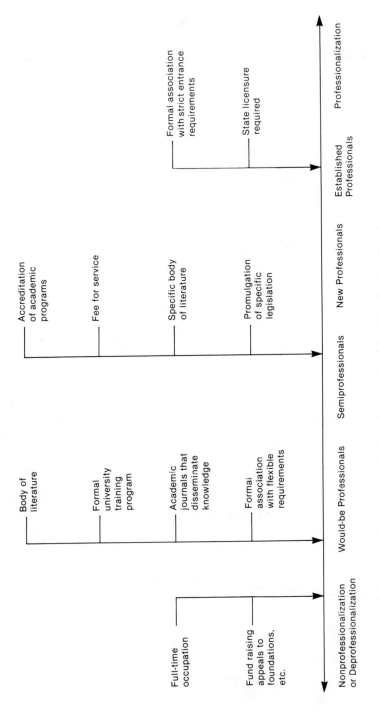

Figure 2–1. A Continuum Model of Professionalization

History of the Professional Field of Gerontology

As with most new fields of study and practice, gerontology was not the result of a conscious plan; it simply developed. As it did so, increasing numbers of professionals and paraprofessionals entered it, some consciously and some by chance. Pioneers in this field found that their interest was regarded as questionable by persons in established professions. For example, James E. Birren, Dean Emeritus of the Andrus Gerontology Center at the University of Southern California, describes the lack of support he received from his college instructors when he indicated his intent to focus his career on research in aging. They cautioned him that this field of study did not exist and that it would never have the legitimacy of established disciplines and professions.

Further, the professionals and paraprofessionals who entered the field in its earlier stages often did so serendipitously (Hirschfield 1979). Typically, a special relationship with an older person led them to explore employment possibilities, they found a job in an agency serving older people, although they may not have sought it, they worked for an agency that began to serve more and more older people, or they got a grant to begin working with older people and later became interested in the area. Thus, current professionals and paraprofessionals in gerontology drifted into the field, and although they may have had some knowledge of and interest in older people, they had little or no formal education in gerontology and no intention originally of making a career of employment in this area.

Many of the professionals and paraprofessionals working in the field of aging today were trained in other fields and continue to think of themselves as belonging to those fields. For example, scientists see their disciplines of origin as their current base—psychology, biology, sociology, political science, economics, and so on. Likewise, liberal gerontologists work within departments of history, English, philosophy, or religion, and practitioners remain social workers, educators, recreators, physicians, or counselors, seeing their service as directed toward older people. Thus, research and service were initially undertaken by nongerontologists who remain involved in the activities of their original profession or discipline and do not immediately describe themselves as gerontologists. However, this situation has been changing in recent years.

As the older population gained visibility, it became clear that the established disciplines and professions were not responding adequately to its needs. Training with regard to aging was not readily available, nor were services designed to address the multiple needs of the elderly. Professionals and paraprofessionals concerned about people in this age group worked at the edges of the human service delivery system, attempting to bridge the gaps. Eventually they realized that a conscious plan for aging service and research was needed, that gerontology could be seen as a field of its own, and that such a perception would benefit both older clients and those interested in helping them.

Some professionals came to the conclusion that as long as gerontology was seen only as an adjunct to other fields, it would be of less importance, never receiving the resources and recognition that it deserved. Professionals and older people began to see that the field of aging needed to be considered legitimate in its own right, a perspective that today is considered necessary to the provision of comprehensive, coordinated services for older people as well as to the ability of multidisciplinary research to unravel the mysteries of aging. However, this realization did not come quickly or universally. In fact, many persons interested in aging still maintain their primary allegiance to their disciplines of origin.

Hirschfield (1979) explored the shift to a view of aging as a separate field by asking a sample of members from the Gerontological Society of America (GSA) and the Western Gerontological Society (WGS) (now the American Society on Aging) to indicate the professional society that received their greatest investment and commitment. Members of sections and organizations that had the strongest orientation toward professional service were the most likely to indicate gerontology as the primary commitment (see table 2–1).

Table 2–1
Percentage of Professional Society Members Indicating a Primary Commitment to Gerontology

Group	Percent Indicating Primary Commitment to Gerontology
GSA, Clinical Medicine and Biological Science Section	33
GSA, Behavioral and Social Science Section	54
GSA, Social Research, Policy and Practice Section	83
WGS	75

Funding supported the adoption of this view. Initial funding for much gerontology research and program operation came not from the organization or institutional budget, but from external sources. The federal government provided most of the research and service dollars, while private philanthropy contributed much to the establishment of services at the local level. Thus, new services were funded that were not just extensions of the traditional programs of other fields, but that involved whole new attempts to help people in need, such as Social Security, Medicare, Foster Grandparents, Retired Senior Volunteer Program, case management, day care, respite care, portal-to-portal transportation, and housing alternatives.

Likewise, in institutions of higher education, new courses dealing with life span development and aging were developed, usually initiated by one interested faculty member, then expanded and organized into a curriculum that resulted in a certificate or concentration in aging. Cooperative, cross-departmental programs were established, often supported by government or foundation funding. The faculty or program developers involved were initially mavericks, either dissatisfied with their current situation or believing in the value of greater concern for the elderly.

Thus, aging services, research, and instruction began to be developed that were different from those offered by existing, traditional service providers. Outside funding helped these to grow, and new agencies and networks were developed. As a result, professionals began to perceive themselves as gerontologists as well as social workers, administrators, nurses, or counselors.

Historical Events That Encouraged the Creation of Professional Gerontology

Some major events were especially influential in developing the field of gerontology. The initial ones can be traced to the Great Depression of the 1930s and its impact on the social and economic welfare of the United States. New programs were initiated in many areas, but the elderly were singled out with the passage of the Social Security Act in 1935. This income maintenance program was initially administered by social workers, but at that time the orientation of social work was largely that of Freudian psychology, which did not fit well with an income maintenance approach or an emphasis on aging. To operate the program successfully, managers and advocates were needed rather than psychoanalytic counselors, so new occupational roles began to develop (Cottrell 1978).

The Housing Act of 1956 provided government support for the first time in independent housing for older persons. Section 202 projects developed across the nation, and jobs for administrators, planners, and architects related to the aging were created.

The Medicare and Medicaid programs of 1965 proved to be a major stimulus to the nursing home industry and encouraged hospitals and home care organizations to provide increased health services to older people. Opportunities for both service providers (physicians, nurses, and therapists) and planners/administrators expanded rapidly.

The Age Discrimination Act of 1967 and the 1978 amendments provided protection for older workers and increased the participation of attorneys, trainers, and job developers in designing means to maintain the productivity and involvement of older workers.

These programs and others began to create an advocacy infrastructure for the field of aging. It was composed of persons employed in the field, groups of activist older people, and legislators and their staff. Together, these groups initiated a long process of raising public consciousness and increasing research and legislation. Public consciousness was raised through the National Conference on Aging, the White House Conferences on Aging, and hundreds of other conferences for professionals, researchers, older people, and advocates. Research, especially that which identified needs and showed results, was helpful in providing the data to support the efforts and verify the results of the new programs being developed.

Legislation, particularly the Older Americans Act, was important because it created another part of the infrastructure, the governmental organization focused totally on older persons. The Older Americans Act was passed in 1965 and has been amended several times since. It has provided the legal basis for creating the National Aging Network, which consists of 57 state and territorial Agencies on Aging, and 666 Area Agencies on Aging, which serve as advocates for older persons and coordinate services to this client group. With over eleven thousand nutrition project sites, and a wide array of publicly and privately supported health and social services, the Aging Network has played a major role in facilitating and operating a variety of programs, such as ombudsman and legal service programs, transportation services, senior centers, day care programs, and respite services. This network has been effectively used to plan and deliver needed services not found elsewhere. Also, it has led to the establishment of the National Association of State Units on Aging and of the National Association of Area Agencies on Aging, organizations committed to local, state, and national cooperation in addressing the problems of older persons.

At the same time that these events were occurring, other developments, primarily at colleges and universities, were establishing a foundation for educating gerontology professionals and researchers. The growth of research funding and learned societies interested in aging encouraged faculty to begin including gerontology content in courses offered within their disciplines. By the 1950s, young investigators interested in the processes of aging were being produced in a few universities. One major event that encouraged this development was the creation of the Interuniversity Council on Social Gerontology, a sixteen-member organization founded in 1957 that produced three handbooks on aging, prepared five course syllabi, and provided training to seventy-five faculty from member institutions (Donahue 1960). New programs began to spring up, such as the Midwest Council for Social Research on Aging in Kansas City, which by 1965 was coordinating doctoral instruction in departments of sociology at a number of midlands universities.

The Older Americans Act also played a role in developing education and training in gerontology. From 1966, funds were made available to colleges and universities for career and short-term training. *Career training* was the term used to describe college and university instruction, typically leading to a master's or bachelor's degree, occasionally in gerontology but more typically in a related profession with an emphasis in gerontology. *Short-term training* usually involved brief, noncredit instruction for currently employed professionals who needed some background on the processes of aging or on the current conditions of older people.

As the field develops, an increasing number of professionals are making longer-term commitments and seeing their future in gerontology. They are likely to seek more extensive training and to advocate for higher entry standards, higher wages, and increased responsibilities.

The 1975 creation of the National Institute on Aging (NIA) added to the federal government an organization that focused on research, research training, and faculty career development. Although research on the processes of aging is still supported by other government and philanthropic agencies, the NIA has become the focal point for both biomedical and social/psychological studies of aging. It has proved to be a powerful stimulus for such studies by identifying Alzheimer's disease as a major target and by encouraging the development of Teaching Nursing Homes for the training of physicians and other professionals. NIA supports research training and faculty career development in a variety of disciplines. Approximately half of the trainees are predoctoral, and half are postdoctoral, with 70 percent of these being in biomedical disciplines and 30 percent in the behavioral and social sciences.

Although the Administration on Aging and the National Institute on Aging are the two federal agencies that have *aging* in their titles, at least forty other federal agencies have some impact on the preparation of personnel for the field of aging (Craig 1980). These do not focus exclusively on gerontology and geriatrics instruction, but at least twenty-one do provide financial support for the development and conduct of instruction in aging. For instance, the Bureau of Health Professions of the Health Resources and Services Administration has supported faculty development, medical residency programs, predoctoral training in medicine, and geriatric instruction for physician assistants and dentists. It is currently supporting geriatric education centers at a number of universities, a variety of projects in nursing education, and the development of geriatric curricula in allied health fields.

The National Institute of Mental Health supports geriatric mental health training for psychiatrists, psychologists, nurses, and social workers. Funds support master's degree, predoctoral, postdoctoral, and faculty development training at a number of colleges and universities and have been instrumental in expanding gerontological instruction within several related professions.

In addition, although it does not fund projects in colleges and universities, the Veterans Administration (VA) has been active for the last ten years in supporting medical fellowships and residencies, interdisciplinary team training, clinical nurse specialist training, master's level social work instruction, and continuing professional education. A wide variety of professionals in training have taken their clinical experience in VA facilities and have received financial support from this organization.

These government agencies, along with support from a variety of foundations, corporations, and private donors, have helped local government agencies, for-profit and nonprofit organizations, and institutions to expand their services to older people and to create many positions that are now increasingly being filled by professionals. Today, the number of these persons exceeds 1.5 million and suggests the large number of occupational roles that have developed in relation to the older population.

Current Perceptions of Gerontology as a Profession

Some persons have contended that gerontology is not and will never be a profession (Loeb 1979). Others have suggested that gerontology is making progress toward becoming a profession (Johnson 1980; Seltzer 1985). Hirschfield and Peterson (1982) have examined gerontology's progress along the continuum and concluded that it now falls somewhere between the semi- and the new profession stages of development. They suggest that gerontology either meets or is close to meeting the requirements of (1) being a full-time occupation, (2) involving long-term dedication to the field, (3) having a specialized body of knowledge, and (4) involving a service orientation, but that it does not as yet appear to meet the criteria of having (5) autonomy of performance, (6) accreditation and licensing, (7) a service monopoly, or (8) a code of ethics.

Hirschfield and Peterson based their conclusions on survey responses from a random sample of 636 members of the gerontological Society of America and the Western Gerontological Society. They reported that 60 percent of the respondents indicated that they considered gerontology to be a profession *currently* and, through response to a series of forced-choice questions, supported further development of the characteristics of a profession.

Of the 608 respondents (92.4 percent of the random sample) approximately 65 percent spent more than half of their professional work week with gerontology-related activities, indicating that gerontology is a full-time occupation for many persons in the field (criterion 1). That percentage had increased substantially, since only 14 percent of the respondents spent a majority of their professional time with older people ten years earlier. This indicates that gerontology is becoming a full-time occupation that is considered the principal source of income for the practitioner.

Although most current practitioners in the field of aging have not completed a gerontology instructional program as preparation, most respondents supported the development of expanded instructional programs (criterion 3). Fifty-four percent supported the idea of offering undergraduate degrees in aging, 82 percent supported the idea of offering master's degrees in aging, and 71 percent supported the development of doctoral degrees in gerontology.

Respondents also saw the need for professional associations to establish entry and practice standards (criterion 6). Eighty-three percent of the respondents indicated that it was an important activity for GSA and WGS to assume leadership in the development of standards for the field, and 71 percent indicated that those societies should develop standards and criteria for licensing persons as gerontologists.

Ninety percent of the respondents indicated support for developing a code of ethics specifying guidelines for individuals working clinically with older adults and saw GSA and WGS as the groups that were most appropriate to develop the standards and process for implementation (criterion 8). Thus, among the respondents in this survey there was general support for development of many professional characteristics as well as acceptance of the idea of gerontology as a profession.

Conclusion

The distinction between a discipline and a profession is important because the orientation that is taken determines in large part the contribution that the field will make to society. If gerontology is a discipline, then the creation and dissemination of knowledge will be its raison d'être and major activity. Although scientific gerontology is a very important orientation and one that must be maintained, it does not appear at present to be the primary concern of most people in the professional field.

Rather, the more pervasive orientation is toward gerontology as knowledge and skill that can be used to help today's older people address the problems that confront them, avoid premature physical and mental decrement, and seek personal growth. This orientation suggests that increased attention will need to be given to meeting all of the criteria of a full profession. Persons desiring to provide services to older people will be expected in the future to acquire some prescribed education before entering the field and to maintain generally accepted standards in the planning and provision of services to older people.

The professional orientation suggests that there is a mission for gerontologists who wish to help improve the quality of life of current and future older persons. Professional gerontology, at least for the next several years, must be viewed as a developing profession that will develop both within other fields and as a separate field with distinct agencies and roles. There are some indications that many current professionals in gerontology already see it as a separate field and identify it as their professional home.

Hirschfield (1979) asked members of the Gerontological Society of America and the Western Gerontological Society to indicate the disciplines/fields with which they had primary identification. Over 25 percent chose gerontology, more than two and one-half times the number who selected the second most frequent choice (social work). This suggests that although much development and consensus building remains to be done before the majority of those working in the field call themselves gerontologists, the profession of gerontology is in the process of being created and already is recognized by many who are working in it.

References

Carr-Saunders, A.M., & Wilson, P.A. (1964). *The professions.* London: Frank Cass & Company.

Cottrell, F. (1978). Gerontology history and development. Paper presented at the Awards Banquet, University of Nebraska at Omaha.

Craig, B. (1980). A preliminary report on the development and implementation of a federal manpower policy for the field of aging. Washington, D.C.: Administration on Aging, Office of Human Development, Department of Health and Human Services.

Donahue, W.T. (1960). Training in social gerontology. *Geriatrics, 15,* 501.

Hirschfield, I.S. (1979). An analysis of gerontology as a multidiscipline or a profession: A 1978 perspective. Unpublished doctoral dissertation, University of Southern California, Los Angeles.

Hirschfield, I.S., & Peterson, D.A. (1982). The professionalization of gerontology. *The Gerontologist, 22,* 215–220.

Johnson, H.R. (1980). Introduction. In C. Tibbitts, H. Friedsam, P. Kerschner, G. Maddox, & H. McClusky (Eds.), *Academic gerontology: Dilemmas of the 1980s.* Ann Arbor: University of Michigan Institute of Gerontology.

Loeb, M.B. (1979). Gerontology is not a profession—the oldest or the youngest. In H.L. Sterns, E.F. Ansello, B.M. Sprouse, & R. Layfield-Faux (Eds.), *Gerontology in higher education: Developing institutional and community strength.* Belmont, Calif.: Wadsworth.

Seltzer, M.M. (1985) Issues of accreditation of academic gerontology programs and credentialing of workers in the field of aging. *Gerontology and Geriatrics Education, 5,* 7–18.

3
Job Roles in the Field of Aging: Opportunities within Established Professions

Persons employed as professionals in the field of aging work in a wide variety of organizations, are involved in a diverse set of actions, and bring very different backgrounds to their work. Their roles are presented here in two categories: (1) job roles within existing professions, discussed in this chapter, and (2) emerging, nontraditional roles, which will be covered in chapter 4. Since people in practically any field might have some contact with or impact on older people, this will not be an exhaustive list. Rather, it will include examples limited to those areas that are most closely related to the existing service delivery system for older people and those fields that are open to students enrolled in gerontology courses.

Few surveys describe the distribution of the various job titles among gerontology professionals. In one such study, Hirschfield (1979) included the collection of data on the roles to which members of the Western Gerontological Society and the Gerontological Society of America allocate the greatest portion of their time. He reported that for a random sample of these members, the administrative role was the most common, while practitioner, teacher, and researcher were also high on the list.

Table 3–1
Percentage of Professional Society Members Allocating Most of Their Time to Various Roles

Roles	Percentage Allocating Greatest Portion of Time to Roles	
	WGS	GSA
Administrator	43	23
Practitioner	11	15
Teacher	12	14
Researcher	4	19
Consultant	8	9
Student	8	8
Planner	6	5
Other	8	7

Members of this same sample group were also asked in what institutional setting they allocated the majority of their time. Colleges and universities received the largest commitment of time from these persons, with social service agencies and government agencies following.

Table 3–2

Percentage of Professional Society Members Allocating Most of Their Time to Various Institutional Settings

Institutional Setting	Percentage Allocating Greatest Portion of Time to Institutional Settings	
	WGS	GSA
Universities and colleges	30	41
Social service agencies	32	16
Government agencies	16	14
Long-term care facilities	6	10
Hospitals	6	6
Private practice	1	5
Private enterprise	4	2
Other	5	6

Many of the members of the GSA were located in colleges and universities and worked primarily in teaching and research roles. WGS members, however, were broadly distributed across a wide range of institutions and roles. Hirschfield's sample probably overrepresents highly educated professionals and may not be completely reflective of all practicing gerontologists. However, it does show the wide distribution of roles and suggests that no one organization or service setting currently houses the majority of gerontologists.

An important question that emerges in relation to Hirschfield's findings is how and where current professionals' time is being allocated in relation to the actual needs of the field. Although a number of attempts have been made to quantify personnel needs in the field of aging, they have been largely unsuccessful. This result has been caused by a number of factors. First, no single agency of the federal government is responsible for collecting and analyzing personnel supply and demand data. Although the Administration on Aging and the National Institute on Aging have undertaken or funded projects in this area, no consistent attempt has been made to determine manpower supply and demand. Second, personnel supply and demand estimates for the field of aging are very difficult to make since most of the personnel do not receive gerontology degrees and most are not employed in organizations that have the term *aging* in their title. Third, attempts to quantify personnel supply and demand have been sporadic, with no consistent plan to generate and use the data. Although a number of reports have been issued, the data that do exist are often noncomparable, so no real progress has been made in developing a methodology or generating data that can be built on in the future.

Fourth, few personnel supply and demand studies on aging have been undertaken by related professional associations. Some fields, such as medicine and nursing, have undergone a number of studies on current and future personnel needs (Kane et al. 1980; Institute of Medicine 1978). Others have received relatively little attention. For instance, the American Public Health Association knows that nine hundred of its thirty thousand members identify themselves with the gerontological health section of that organization, but it otherwise has no data on the number or percent of public health personnel who work with older people (de la Puente 1986). Likewise, the American Sociological Association (Huber 1986), the Clinical Sociology Association (Clark 1986), the American Alliance for Health, Physical Education, Recreation, and Dance (Ciszek 1986), the American Home Economics Association (McFadden 1986), the American Bar Association (Coleman 1986), public administration (Birren and Hirschfield 1977), and occupational therapy (Davis 1984) have no information on the proportion of their members who work primarily with older persons.

Gerontology Personnel Supply and Demand

One approach to gaining some understanding of gerontology personnel supply has been to identify the extent and level of current instruction in gerontology at American colleges and universities. Nearly forty different studies of gerontology instruction have been located; they confirm that growth in the number of instructional programs is extensive.

To supplement these existing reports, the Association for Gerontology in Higher Education and the University of Southern California undertook a comprehensive survey of gerontology instruction in 1985–86. A portion of the findings are described in chapter 5 of this book, but some of the data are applicable here. They indicated that over 320,000 students nationwide have completed at least one credit course in gerontology, and 191,000 have completed noncredit workshops or seminars during the past twenty years. This does not suggest that over a half million people are "trained" in gerontology, but it does indicate that many college students and current practitioners are gaining some knowledge of the academic field of gerontology and that the number of colleges and universities offering this instruction continues to expand.

However, this research fails to answer several questions regarding gerontology training: for instance, whether it has a liberal, scientific, or professional emphasis; in what professional fields it is offered; or at what levels it is available. Neither do the data provide much insight into the consistency of the instructional programs. For example, a recent survey by the Council on Social Work Education (Nelson and Schneider 1984) reported that forty-one schools of social work offered a "concentration in gerontology" but did not indicate how much course and field work that included or whether the term was used consistently among the reporting institutions.

The lack of information on personnel supply is comparable to the meager information on various subgroups of personnel. For instance, few studies have examined the extent to which minority individuals are being prepared to enter the field of aging. In 1980, the Administration on Aging contracted with the EMAY Corporation to explore this area. After explaining that the data available were neither comprehensive nor extensive, the researchers reported that over 90 percent of the minority students in gerontology instructional programs were black and that other minorities were not numerous in any region, field, or level of education in gerontology (Craig 1980).

In addition to these studies that assess the *supply* of personnel from gerontological education programs, a number of attempts have been made to quantify requirements for gerontology personnel in the workplace. This is difficult to do, however, because only rough estimates of currently active personnel exist, and little is known about labor market participation rates and employment settings.

Requirements for professionals can be expressed as *demand,* the number of individuals that employers will hire given certain economic conditions and consumer preferences, and *need,* the total number of personnel needed to provide a level of health service judged adequate or desirable by experts (Bureau of Health Professions 1984). Neither demand nor need information is available in most areas of the field of aging, and estimates of the number of personnel required tend to be based on expert opinion and subjective rather than quantitative data. However, those reports that do exist provide some insight into current and future requirements for gerontology professionals.

The first of these reports, undertaken by Surveys and Research Corporation (1969), collected data in the areas of retirement housing, recreation, and state and federal government employment. In addition, it collated existing data from several relevant fields. The final report supplied estimates for personnel in eighteen related fields, including nursing, nursing home administration, social work, recreation, and housing administration. Personnel who worked with the elderly composed about 14 percent of all workers in these eighteen areas. The report indicated that approximately 330,000 people were employed in programs that exclusively or primarily served older people, half of these being nurses' aides in long-term care settings. It was estimated that by 1980, two to three times this many people would be needed, with needed increases in the number of retirement housing administrators approaching

800 percent, recreation leaders 200 percent, and long-term care personnel over 100 percent.

The most ambitious attempt to estimate aging personnel supply and demand was undertaken between 1975 and 1978 by the Labor Department's Bureau of Labor Statistics (BLS). With funding from the Administration on Aging, BLS carried out preliminary investigations in several areas that resulted in five analytical reports published by the Administration on Aging, ten career counseling brochures, and articles in six separate issues of the Department of Labor's *Occupational Outlook Quarterly* (Craig 1980). The conclusions drawn by the BLS reports were not very optimistic about the availability of employment in the field of aging at the time the studies were conducted. However, they did expect continued future growth in the number of jobs.

Other studies (for example, Birren and Sloan 1977; National Association of Social Workers 1983) have painted a more optimistic picture for gerontology personnel in search of jobs, with many openings projected within already existing professions. Here we will discuss only those job roles that frequently involve work with older populations.

Roles within Other Professions

Nurses. The field of nursing appears to provide the largest number of positions that relate to older people. The most recent attempt to examine supply and demand in this area of gerontology service is the National Institute on Aging (NIA) *Report on Education and Training in Geriatrics and Gerontology* (1984). In considering the future need for gerontological nursing personnel, this report indicated that need will increase rapidly in the coming years. At present there are approximately 100,000 registered nurses (RNs) employed in nursing homes and extended care facilities, about 8 percent of all employed RNs. If the current patterns of staffing continue, the growth in the population over age eighty will mean that over 150,000 RNs will be needed in nursing homes by 1990; furthermore, that number will need to increase to 250,000 by the year 2000.

About three of every five jobs in the nursing home industry are related to nursing, where the nurse in a nursing home is likely to have major responsibilities for the care of older persons and to have access to fewer backup resources than would be the case in an acute care hospital. Physicians are generally not on the premises, and nurses are the only licensed health workers allowed to administer medications and assess changes in a patient's condition. Nurses frequently have assumed administrative roles in nursing homes, serving as assistant administrators or directors of nursing in addition to being nursing home administrators.

Although the majority of positions are available in nursing homes, geron-tological nurses are also found in hospitals, community service, and instruc-tion. Nurses also provide basic health care to individuals in their homes, typ-ically through public health or visiting nurse programs and hospital outreach services. For example, a nurse may visit the home of a recently discharged hospital patient, provide assistance to diabetics needing injections, or super-vise home health care aides. In 1974, over 2,300 agencies were certified as home health agencies under the Medicare program, and another 2,000 pro-vided similar services but did not participate in Medicare. In 1984, approx-imately 53,600 registered nurses were employed in community health nurs-ing, and that number will need to double by 1990 and double again by the year 2,000 (NIA 1984).

Allied Health Professionals. A variety of health personnel are included in the category of allied health professionals. Most of these occupational groups developed between 1940 and 1970 as a result of the explosion of medical knowledge and the rapid introduction of new technologies and services (Bureau of Health Professions 1984). They include technologists, therapists, and others who perform relatively high-level health care functions, assistants whose duties vary in complexity, and aides who perform routine supportive services. Only a few of the professions in this group provide special services to older persons, and several of these—such as art, dance, educational, and music therapy—are such new professions or are so limited in the number of practitioners that few data are available on them. Therefore, only three will be discussed here: physical, occupational, and speech therapists.

Occupational therapists provide services to persons of all ages who are physically, psychologically, and developmentally disabled. They assist patients in achieving the maximum level of independent living by developing those capacities that remain after disease, accident, or deformity. There are two levels of personnel: occupational therapists and occupational therapy assistants. Of the approximately 38,600 licensed occupational therapists today, 30 percent work primarily with older people and another 20 percent work part-time with older people (Davis 1986). This number needs to increase by 900 percent as the number of persons over the age of seventy-five increases (Ellis 1986). Those in gerontological capacities are usually in the roles of administrator of an occupational therapy (OT) department, staff occupa-tional therapist, or consultant in private practice. Most work in nursing homes, but acute care hospitals and home health agencies are also likely orga-nizational bases (Davis 1984).

Physical therapy is concerned with the rehabilitation of individuals who have been physically disabled by disease or accident or who were born with a physical handicap (Alperin and Alperin 1980). Treatment involves regulated exercise, water, light, electricity, and heat. Entry to the field of physical therapy is made through the completion of a four-year bachelor's degree in the field, a twelve- to sixteen-month certificate for persons holding a bachelor's degree in other fields, and a master's degree for those with a bachelor's degree in related fields. All fifty states require physical therapists to be licensed (U.S. Department of Labor 1984). Over 43,000 physical therapists are employed in the United States today, approximately 8 percent in nursing homes where they primarily serve older people, and 47 percent in acute care facilities where a portion of the patients are older (U.S. Department of Labor 1984). In 1980, the Bureau of Labor Statistics estimated that the number of physical therapists required for good care to older people in nursing homes was 9,300, nearly triple the 3,440 employed in nursing homes at that time (National Clearinghouse on Aging 1976).

Many speech-language-hearing professionals work with older people who have experienced communication disorders that significantly curtail their social relationships and limit their capacity to carry out everyday life activities. In 1980, 20 percent of the speech-impaired individuals and 43 percent of the hearing-impaired individuals in the United States were over age sixty-five (Fein 1984). In 1984, persons sixty-five and over composed 14 percent of the caseload for speech-language pathologists and 32 percent for audiologists, indicating that the elderly are underserved compared with other age groups. At the present time the supply of speech-language pathologists and audiologists is not sufficient to meet the demand. The growing older population is expected to increase employment opportunities for these professionals well into the twenty-first century (Spahr 1985).

Physician's Assistants. As the cost of medical care has increased, the service delivery system has developed new roles that allow physicians to extend their services. One of these roles is that of the physician's assistant, a skilled health practitioner qualified by academic and clinical experience to provide patient service under the supervision and direction of a physician (Bureau of Health Professions 1984). As of January 1983, approximately 16,400 physician's assistants had graduated from fifty-four accredited programs and had obtained formal certification. Up to 95 percent of these persons are involved in patient care, with 54 percent working in family practice. As their numbers have grown, physician's assistants have become more common in the provision of service to the elderly, working in nursing homes where they can expand the quality and quantity of services provided to patients. A new trend is to have full-time physician's assistants in long-term care facilities, frequently replacing foreign house officers (Bureau of Health Professions 1984).

Physicians. Physicians are responsible for the provision of preventive, diagnostic, treatment, and rehabilitative services to the elderly (NIA 1984). In order for many health services to be covered by Medicare or Medicaid, the applicable service must be deemed necessary and be ordered by the physician. This makes the medical doctor a key individual in providing older people access to health and medical services. Stulz (1984) reported that "currently 30 percent of the practice of internists and medical subspecialists is devoted to the elderly and this may increase to 50 percent within the next twenty years." Until recently, few medical schools offered gerontology or geriatric instruction, but courses and clinical residencies have expanded rapidly since 1980. However, it is expected that for many years to come there will be a critical undersupply of geriatric physicians—both those who directly provide services to the elderly and medical faculty who train new physicians and conduct aging-related research.

The Rand Corporation undertook a study of supply and demand of geriatric physicians in 1980 (Kane et al. 1980). It reported that in 1977 there were 715 geriatricians in the United States, and that this number would have to grow to approximately 8,000 by the year 2000. The need for this huge growth is based on a different assumption than that adopted in the BLS studies, which viewed the future openings in this field as minimal. BLS staff assumed that funds would need to be available to employ additional staff, and they could not foresee the likelihood of those funds' being available. Thus, they assumed the positions might be needed but would not be created. The Rand group assumed that funds would come from the government, insurance, or personal payment and so reported on the need for rather than the likelihood of actual positions' being created.

Teachers and Researchers. Researchers and college teachers of gerontology typically are employed in one of the traditional disciplines: biology, psychology, sociology, political science, or economics. Although the number of college faculty is not expanding nationally, positions in gerontology continue to be advertised as new programs are started and current faculty retire. A recent Rand study (Kane et al. 1980) estimated that 1,700–2,600 basic and applied researchers are needed in geriatrics. If the need for researchers in gerontology had been added into this estimate, the number would be significantly higher.

Preparation for research and teaching typically involves the completion of a doctoral degree, although many community college faculty find that a master's degree is sufficient for teaching at that level. Gerontology is typically taught within the traditional disciplines, though some institutions do have gerontology degree or certificate programs. At the present time, doctoral degrees in gerontology do not exist, so graduate training in a related field is expected.

Social Workers. Social workers seek to promote the dignity and well-being of all citizens and have found career opportunities in many places in the field of gerontology (Schneider 1984). They are found providing direct services in multipurpose centers, hospices, public welfare agencies, Veterans Administration facilities, and nursing homes. They are also found in planning, advocacy, and administration positions, and in teaching and research. The direct service role frequently involves casework, counseling, information provision, referral, financial planning, and placement in, aiding adjustment to, and discharge from hospitals and nursing homes. Of approximately 115,000 practicing social workers in 1984, 5,750 were employed in roles directly related to older persons (NIA 1984).

Although the BLS study did not estimate the number of social workers primarily serving the elderly or make estimates of future demand, it did report on the convening of a meeting of national leaders in this area to discuss opportunities for social workers in aging. These leaders perceived that gerontological social workers were being paid less and had fewer career ladders and less job security than social workers in other positions (National Clearinghouse on Aging 1979b). However, empirically based estimates of future demand are much more optimistic, suggesting that the number of geriatric social workers will need to increase tremendously in order to meet the needs of the growing older population.

In 1982, Clyde Helms, president of an occupational forecasting company, predicted that by 1990 there would be 700,000 jobs available for geriatric social workers (National Association of Social Workers 1983). His estimates were based on population changes rather than on existing job categories, and he suggested that creative responses will be needed to fill the developing job opportunities in relation to the older population.

Recreation Personnel. Therapeutic recreation workers and activity coordinators design and carry out programs that enhance leisure time. Such programs include arts and crafts, instructional programs, discussion groups, exercise and dance programs, music, travel, and sports. Activity coordinators are often responsible for developing volunteer services, including the recruitment, training, and supervision of volunteers who work in the institution or agency. In 1975, over 90 percent of all nursing homes had activity coordinators, either full- or part-time (Kahl 1976). Skilled nursing homes are required to have an activity program that is conducted or overseen by a staff member or consultant trained in this area.

Recreation personnel can be divided into two categories: activity directors and administrators. The activity director is the frontline leader who develops and carries out the recreation activity. This individual typically has less experience and a lower educational level than the program coordinator/administrator. The administrator typically is in a consultative or supervisory capacity designing programs, overseeing the work of the activity director, and seeking the financial resources and physical settings that enable the enhancement of recreational programs.

In 1979, the BLS reported on the availability of jobs as recreation workers with older persons (Wash 1979). The report focused on qualitative statements, since current and historical data were not available to indicate how many recreation workers were employed in settings that served elderly people. Most were doubtless employed in institutions such as nursing homes, but the number involved in community-based programs was impossible to estimate. A meeting of faculty and practitioners in this area indicated that a more than adequate supply of trained recreation workers existed at that time. However, the situation resulted more from the lack of strict professional and educational standards for the area, the recent sizable increase in the number of parks and recreation graduates, and the austerity of budgets adopted by many local government agencies than from a true assessment of need. It was noted that a nationwide shortage existed of college professors trained to teach courses in recreation and aging. Further, educators in the field report that recreation graduates with a background in aging have done better in the job market than have graduates in most other parts of the recreation field (Wash 1979).

Counselors and Psychologists. Counselors are heavily involved in providing direct service to older people. In some states, licenses are required to conduct family counseling, which often includes work with older people. In most states, however, it is possible for a person to do counseling without a specific license. Counselors are found in public and private family service agencies, mental health centers, counseling centers, hospitals, long-term care facilities, and multipurpose senior centers. The role performed by the counselor is likely to vary depending on the nature of the problem faced by the older person, but generally support and therapy are offered on a one-to-one or small group basis.

Psychologists have a long history of involvement with aging. In the past, psychologists interested in aging were most likely to be researchers or university faculty who explored developmental changes (sensory, perceptual, and cognitive) over the life course. More recently, clinical or counseling psychologists have become involved in providing one-to-one and small group services to older people. A clinical psychologist typically has a Ph.D. and concentrates on the administration and interpretation of psychological tests. In the field of aging clinical psychologists are also involved in therapy, consultation, research, education, and administration. They are typically employed in private practice clinics, hospitals, and mental health centers. Although there is a critical need for them in nursing homes, few of them are found in this setting.

Birren and Sloan (1977) reported on manpower and training needs for the field of mental health and aging. They estimated the number of older people who would be likely to need mental health services in the future and concluded that there was a severe lack of trained personnel for mental health positions with the elderly. They suggested that to begin meeting these needs, it would be necessary to increase the number of personnel trained in gerontology from twenty psychiatrists in 1977 to one thousand in 1985; from one hundred clinical psychologists to two thousand; and from fifty psychiatric nurses to four thousand.

As the size of the older population increases, more mental health services will be demanded, and psychologists and psychiatrists will supply them. This is possible since many mental health practitioners are in private practice or are employed by institutions and clinics that can modify staffing as services are needed. In contrast, most social workers, recreators, nursing home staff, and home health personnel are not self-employed, and new jobs will become available only through the creation of new government programs—not a likely event in the current era of budget reductions.

Conclusion

Job roles in the field of aging are not limited to those described in this chapter. Many other roles exist; especially common are those such as the nurses' aide, home health worker, social service aide, home chore worker, and recreation assistant. These roles are more numerous than those that require extensive formal education at the associate, bachelor's, or master's degree level, but they are of less direct interest to persons who are undertaking gerontology education in order to enter the field.

Many of the job roles in the field of aging that require educational preparation are in traditional professions, such as social work, nursing, and medicine. Access to these jobs is restricted to persons who have successfully completed a specific educational program and have been licensed or certified. This means that persons interested in employment in these licensed roles will need to become social workers, nurses, or physicians before they can serve the aged. This is the route that many students choose, and it is in keeping with a view of gerontology as an area of specialization within already existing professions.

On the other hand, many positions do not fit into a distinct, traditional profession. To date, most of these roles do not require background in a specific educational area or a particular credential. These jobs—administrators, planners, service providers, program developers, evaluators, and consultants—are open to anyone and offer a great array of opportunities for professional growth and service to the older population. Their character and availability is discussed in the next chapter.

References

Alperin, S., & Alperin, M. (1980). *120 careers in the health care field.* Cambridge, Mass.: Ballinger Publishing Company.

Birren, J.E., & Hirschfield, I.S. (1977). *An analysis of professional education in the state of California for services to retired and aged.* Los Angeles: Andrus Gerontology Center, University of Southern California.

Birren, J.E., & Sloan, R.B. (1977). *Manpower and training needs in mental health and illness of the aging.* Los Angeles: Andrus Gerontology Center, University of Southern California.

Bureau of Health Professions. (1984). *Report to the President and Congress on the status of health personnel in the United States, May 1984.* Washington, D.C.: Heath Resources and Services Administration, Public Health Service, Department of Health and Human Services.

Ciszek, R.A. (February 3, 1986). Personal communication.

Clark, E.J. (February 3, 1986). Personal communication.

Coleman, N. (February 14, 1986). Personal communication.

Craig, B. (1980). *A preliminary report on the development and implementation of a federal manpower policy for the field of aging.* Washington, D.C.: Administration on Aging, Office of Human Development Services, Department of Health and Human Services.

Davis, L. (1986). Introduction. In L. Davis and M. Kirkland (Eds.), *The role of occupational therapy with the elderly.* Rockville, Md.: The American Occupational Therapy Association.

Davis, L. (1984). Personal communication.

de la Puente, J. (January 8, 1986). Personal communication.

Ellis, N.B. (1986). Foreword. In L. Davis & M. Kirkland (Eds.) *The role of occupational therapy with the elderly.* Rockville, Md.: The American Occupational Therapy Association.

Fein, J.J. (1984). On aging. *Asha, 26,* 25.

Hirschfield, I.S. (1979). An analysis of gerontology as a multidiscipline or a profession: A 1978 perspective. Unpublished doctoral dissertation, University of Southern California.

Huber, B.J. (January 29, 1986). Personal communication.

Institute of Medicine. (1978). *Report of a study: Aging and medical education.* Washington, D.C.: National Academy of Sciences.

Kahl, A. (1976). Jobs with service programs. *Occupational Outlook Quarterly, 20,* 13–29.

Kane, R.L. , Solomon, D.H., Beck, J.C., Keeler, E., and Kane, R.A. (1980). *Geriatrics in the United States: Manpower projections and training considerations.* Santa Monica, Calif.: Rand Corporation.

McFadden, J.R. (February 11, 1986). Personal communication.

National Association of Social Workers. (1983). Geriatric social work picked as growth area. *NASW News,* 3.

National Clearinghouse on Aging. (1976). *AoA occasional papers in gerontology: No. 1. Manpower needs in the field of aging: The nursing home industry.* Washington, D.C.: Government Printing Office.

National Clearinghouse on Aging. (1979b) *AoA occasional papers in gerontology: No. 4: Employment and training issues in social work with the elderly.* Washington, D.C.: Administration on Aging, Office of Human Development Services, Department of Health and Human Services.

National Institute on Aging. (1984). *Report on education and training in geriatrics and gerontology.* Washington, D.C.: National Institute on Aging, Public Health Service, U.S. Department of Health and Human Services.

Nelson, G.M., & Schneider, R.L. (1984). *The current status of gerontology in graduate social work education.* New York: Council on Social Work Education.

Schneider, R.L. (Ed.) (1984). *The integration of gerontology into social work educational curricula.* Washington, D.C.: Council on Social Work Education.

Spahr, F.T. (October, 1985). Personal communication.

Stulz, B.M. (1984). Preventative health care for the elderly. *Western Journal of Medicine, 141,* 832–845.

Surveys and Research Corporation. (1969). *The demand for personnel and training in the field of aging.* Washington, D.C.: Administration on Aging, Office of Human Development Services, Department of Health, Education and Welfare.

U.S. Department of Labor. (1984). *Occupational outlook handbook.* Washington, D.C.: Government Printing Office.

Wash, P. (1979). *Employment issues in recreation for the elderly.* Washington, D.C.: Bureau of Labor Statistics, Department of Labor.

4

Job Roles for Gerontologists: New Opportunities in a Developing Profession

The occupational roles described in the preceding chapter have existed for some time and can be readily understood by persons familiar with health, housing, and human service programs in the United States. They fit within the widely recognized patterns of jobs related to service occupations, and, although the range is probably somewhat broader than would be expected in any of the individual professions, they are defined as part of the existing professions. Other occupational roles are less well developed but also provide opportunities for people seeking employment in the field of aging. These new job roles are not readily categorized into any of the existing professions. Some of these roles are only now becoming widespread, and most do not have specific training programs for preparing professionals or the licensing or certification requirements of the traditional professions. Thus, the existence of these roles suggests that the field of gerontology is beginning to develop as a distinct area.

Opportunities in Developed Areas

Opportunities exist in the areas of administration, planning, and the development of services for older persons. Professionals enter these fields from a variety of backgrounds and find the opportunities for advancement very open. Because these roles have both stability and openness, they are often considered by persons interested in entering the field of aging.

Nursing Home Administrators. Although nursing home administrators must be licensed, most states have only recently required that the individual complete a formal educational program to be eligible for this role. Thus, the background of current administrators varies substantially, with some having little or no college education. Many of those who do hold a college degree received it from such programs as business administration, public administration, planning, social science, nursing, the ministry, or the humanities. As licensing becomes more restrictive, future administrators are more likely to be graduates of formal administrator training programs.

Nursing home administrators spend a great deal of their time making policies, evaluating programs, planning budgets, assuring compliance with government regulations, and overseeing staff (Bolton and Scott 1979). As the size of nursing homes has grown (as measured by the number of beds for residents), many nursing homes have been acquired by large companies that own a chain of homes. Communication and planning within the corporation, then, take an increasing amount of the administrator's time.

For the most part, each of the twenty-three thousand nursing homes in the United States has an administrator, and those with more than seventy-five beds usually have an assistant administrator or an administrative intern as well. This means that there are nearly fifty thousand jobs in this area at the present time. New nursing homes are likely to be larger than those of the past, and more older homes are being purchased by health care companies and expanded to increase the cost efficiency. Thus, these opportunities for highly trained administrators are expected to continue to increase.

Housing Managers. The development of housing for older people who want to maintain an independent life-style has brought with it employment opportunities for professionals who administer the operation of large apartment/ independent living facilities. Many of these retirement facilities provide several levels of care, requiring the manager to have a good understanding of the different needs and wants of older residents, as well as a familiarity with many aspects of facilities management and human services.

No licensing exists for housing managers (unless their facility includes a nursing home), so their backgrounds vary a great deal. As the size and complexity of these facilities and their programs have grown, some education and administrative experience are increasingly required of housing managers, but openings are still being filled by persons with preparation in a number of related fields. Many of the available positions in this area are found in private, profit-making corporations that are building luxury accommodations for older people with substantial resources. The demand for professionals with good administrative and financial skills and some knowledge of the older consumer is likely to remain strong for some time to come.

Senior Center Administrators. Multipurpose senior centers are community facilities that provide social, referral, recreational, travel, nutritional, and educational services to older people. Most senior centers include a facility for social events and services, although many also use satellite sites to increase accessibility for older people in the community. Many existing centers are small, having a staff of three or four people, and rely on the service of a large number of volunteers. The administrator oversees the whole program and frequently is involved in leading some of the activities as well.

There is no licensing of senior center administrators, and few educational programs exist to prepare persons for this role. Current administrators are likely to have a background in recreation, social work, or another human service field, although some doubtless have been promoted into their position with little or no formal educational preparation.

Administrators of Adult Day Care. Adult day care centers have developed in the past fifteen years as a way to provide services to older persons who do not need institutionalization but who can benefit from custodial and rehabilitative care. Some families are not able to provide round-the-clock care, and others use the day care service as a way of accessing a variety of services at one location. Centers vary in size from a few clients to seventy or more, and administrators are responsible for planning and managing these support programs, as well as for assuring compliance with all local, state, and federal regulations. As in other small organizations, the administrator often is involved in supervising and training staff, maintaining the financial records, overseeing volunteers, managing public relations, and doing case management of the participants (National Institute on Adult Daycare 1984). Day care directors typically have backgrounds in nursing, public health, social work, or community services, but persons with gerontology education are increasingly finding jobs in this area.

Administrators of Public Agencies. Many public agencies facilitate and support the provision of services to older people, ranging from health and mental health to employment, housing, education, recreation, social services, transportation, and financial planning. These agencies include the U.S. Administration on Aging, offices on aging, which are a part of the government of each state, and the 666 local Area Agencies on Aging, which are responsible for local planning and service coordination. Although these agencies actually offer a relatively minor proportion of the services, they do provide financial support for many of the services with funds from the federal government, through the state, to the local agency. Administrators of public agencies vary in their skills and backgrounds, but most engage in the general process of organizational development, administration of staff and programs, oversight of the complex relationships with other agencies, and involvement in the political process that results in government funding and regulations. As the amount of funding has grown, so has the complexity of dealing with fund securing, reporting, affirmative action, staff development, community relations, and oversight by elected officials. Most current administrators find it useful to have had some education in public administration or business administration, but many have come to their jobs from direct service roles and have acquired their knowledge of management while on the job. Currently, government programs are stable or shrinking rather than growing rapidly. This means that the demand for public administrators is weak and is expected to remain that way for several years.

Opportunities in Newly Developing Areas

Newly developing job roles frequently go unrecognized because they have emerged only recently in response to a perceived need. Some of these roles exist within the context of the traditional employment settings—nursing homes, hospitals, social service programs, and educational institutions—while others are outside traditional organizational contexts.

These roles frequently have vague titles, and in some cases the responsibilities have developed around the skills and interests of the incumbent. For example, some of these roles are created by individuals who have particular interests and use them to modify old roles or develop new approaches to situations. In such cases, the role may change substantially or disappear when that individual leaves. Salaries vary as much as the responsibilities. Some are at the level of part-time, temporary employment, and some involve very high levels of compensation.

The descriptions of job roles that follow are based primarily on the employment experience of former students of the Andrus Gerontology Center, but these descriptions seem to be generalizable to professionals who have graduated from many other gerontology instructional programs, as well as to those with no educational background in aging.

These job roles do not fit into any neat set of categories, so it is impossible to describe the current supply or demand for personnel. In order to organize this chapter, the roles are presented in the categories of entrepreneurship, new areas of education and training, planning, service, program development, and employment. Some of the job roles overlap two or more of these categories, and those in the grouping "Other Job Roles" do not fit well within any.

Entrepreneurship. Many new job roles in gerontology involve offering consultation or assistance outside the agencies and organizations of the service delivery system. Persons in these positions typically are not staff members of organizations or institutions but are self-employed, using a fee-for-service approach to helping older people. Probably the largest number of persons in this area are case managers, who provide assistance such as information and referral, brokering of services, advocacy, and counseling to older persons or their families. Those in this role are growing in numbers and importance as the social service and health delivery systems become more and more complex and specialized. The case manager often helps the older person to discover and use appropriately social and health delivery services.

In some cases, these case managers work with a team of professionals (physicians, therapists, psychologists) to assess needs and then provide or locate appropriate services. When this approach is successfully carried out, it eventually brings about the creation of a new organization designed specifically to identify and meet the special needs of the older person. Other case managers work alone, receiving referrals from hospitals, nursing homes, families, or other helpers. Their role is to assist the older client in determining and accessing the best services at the best prices within the community.

Other entrepreneurs are self-employed consultants who provide services to hospitals, nursing homes, or community agencies. They frequently fill gaps for organizations that do not have full-time staff available to handle these services. For the institution, this situation is less expensive than hiring a new staff member, and for the gerontologist it provides the freedom and flexibility that some people seek. In some cases, the gerontologist helps the institution design and implement a new program, such as group health services, marketing to older people, or activities or education for older persons. In addition, evaluation of services is also frequently done by consultants.

New Areas of Education and Training. Many gerontologists find themselves involved in the instructional side of the field. They may perform this role as consultants, but usually teaching is developed as a role for a staff member of an organization such as a hospital, nursing home, health care network, or social service agency. These organizations have discovered that their services can be maximized by helping older clients and their families to develop appropriate compliance strategies, to adopt new behaviors that will be supportive of personal health, and to gain an understanding of other options that may be pursued in the future. Leading workshops, working with support groups, and offering a variety of health promotion classes are typical roles for these gerontologists.

Training of paraprofessionals and professionals is another rapidly developing role. Since so few practitioners, especially those at the lower levels of preparation, have any formal background in gerontology, the need exists for orientation to the characteristics of older people, to the modifications of service that need to be made, and to the network of services that exists for older people. Although they do not intend it, many gerontology professionals find that they are considered the experts on aging so are expected to share their expertise with others regularly. For some persons, this instructional role is carried out at a community college or at a university, but most teach within community organizations and institutions.

Planning. Many professionals who are not in direct service roles have the responsibility of leading agencies and organizations in determining future strategies, assessing competing approaches, and exploring the political and social impact of proposed projects. Planners may have degrees from departments of urban planning, but they may also come from other backgrounds that provide them with analytic skills and projection techniques useful in charting the future course of their agencies. Although their roles are so diverse that no specific supply and demand estimates are available, most state units on aging and many agencies on aging have professional staff with the title of planner.

Service. Social service and health care for the elderly are provided by a wide variety of agencies, organizations, and programs that have diverse purposes, client groups, funding sources, and philosophies (Kahl 1976). Many of these services are performed by persons from related professions, but others are performed by individuals who are not social workers, nurses, or therapists, but who see themselves as persons working in the field of aging regardless of their background or educational preparation.

Service programs include such areas as home health care, homemaker services, home repair, telephone reassurance, senior center services, information and referral, transportation, education, nutrition, legal services, housing services, ombudsman services, and advocacy. Many agencies and organizations offering these services originally received funding from the U.S. Administration on Aging and became part of the National Aging Network. Subsequently, many have secured other funding from such local agencies as United Way, from foundations, or through direct payment by clients or third-party payers.

The number of new service programs for the elderly is truly amazing; especially numerous are those designed to serve older persons in their own homes rather than in institutional settings. Since this is a new approach, these programs offer substantial opportunities for innovative gerontologists to create their own jobs for serving older people. For example, some have developed and are operating shared housing projects, health maintenance organizations, home health care, counseling services, travel services, guardianship services, and outreach. Hospitals and nursing homes in search of clients have developed many outreach and in-home services as well as day treatment facilities. Health maintenance organizations are doing much planning, program development, and evaluation, and educational institutions are offering many opportunities for older people.

Program Development. Although many of their duties are similar to those of administrators and planners, program developers typically work at a different level and have a different orientation in their work. They are generally staff of existing agencies who are given or who volunteer for the assignment of planning and implementing a new service or project. They have much more direct responsibility than does the administrator, since the program planner typically moves from the idea stage to reality through personal planning and heavy personal involvement. The program planner typically writes the proposal to secure funding, organizes the advisory committee, selects the staff, and performs the service during its early months of operation.

Some program planners eventually move into administrative roles, but currently they are closer to the clients and are responsible for only one project or service rather than several, as may be the case with administrators. Program planners may have a variety of titles and educational backgrounds, but they are usually visionaries, willing to devote long hours to the job and dedicated to creating a new service that will be of benefit to older people.

This role may sound somewhat vague, but it is very real to recent graduates of gerontology educational programs. They frequently find that they must create their own roles if they are to work with older people in the ways they prefer. Rather than finding the ideal job, they accept a traditional one that has the potential to become the ideal. Over time, they clarify their priorities, and when the opportunity presents itself, they take the initiative to build a new program around their interests and beliefs. Thus, the program planner role is especially meaningful to gerontology professionals, and it should be seen as a stepping stone to leadership in service to older people.

Employment. The trend toward early retirement means that many people in their fifties and sixties leave the work force before the traditional retirement age. For some, retirement is everything they expected, and they have no desire to return to work. Others, however, miss the activity, status, and income associated with employment and seek new work opportunities. Many gerontologists are currently involved in helping these individuals gain the skills and access necessary to secure part- or full-time employment. With government support through the Joint Partnership Training Act (JPTA) and private funding, second-career centers that provide training and job placement have grown rapidly.

Other Job Roles. Unmentioned so far are those roles developed by gerontologists that do not fit into the above categories. For example, roles are available for professionals skilled in applied research to design increasingly sophisticated evaluations of community and institutional services. These persons may be employed by the service agency, but they are most frequently found in educational institutions or consulting firms. Whatever their organizational base, they are crucial to the generation of data on the impact of programs and their financial viability.

Roles preparing printed or audio-visual material on aging are also developing as the demand for both popular books and educational materials rapidly increases. Likewise, financial planning, retirement preparation, and career counseling for middle-aged persons is growing both in corporate settings and in educational and service organizations since the demand for public information and preparation is increasing. Professionals in these latter roles may consider themselves educators or they may see themselves primarily as being in the area of human resource development concentrating their efforts on helping employees with benefits and providing counseling.

Finally, there is on the horizon a group of jobs for persons with knowledge and skill in gerontology which relates to the consumer preferences of older people. More and more companies are marketing products and services to older people, and as they do, there will be roles for gerontologists who can identify the wants of older people and the methods that will effectively convey information about products and services.

Approaches to Securing Nontraditional Gerontology Employment

Nontraditional gerontology employment, like that just described, does not involve generalized job descriptions and is not secured through listed position vacancies in the help-wanted ads. The jobs do exist, but acquiring them frequently seems more closely associated with luck than with the instructional program that is completed by the student gerontologist. However, as many successful people have pointed out, luck is largely the result of planning, perseverance, and hard work, and this is clearly the case with nontraditional jobs in gerontology. Since many of these jobs will go to new professionals entering the field, it is the responsibility of these gerontology students and their faculty mentors to see that the elements are properly arranged to result in "lucky" job placements.

To achieve this result involves a series of six career-planning steps that prepare the student to optimize the likelihood of acquiring the best job. The first step is self-assessment, a careful exploration of the student's interests, preferences, aptitudes, abilities, previous work experience, personal traits, and preferred life-style. When clarified, these factors should be compared with various categories of job roles in the field of aging so that the areas of best fit can be ascertained and preliminary decisions made on the best part of the field to explore.

The second step is the acquisition of occupational information about various job roles and opportunities. It may mean deciding on direct service versus administration, or employment in an organization rather than entrepreneurship. The student can gain information by meeting program alumni, talking with professionals at meetings and conferences, taking part-time employment, and most importantly, working in internships. Experience has shown that the internship is the most decisive factor in the acquisition of employment, and the careful selection of an internship role complementary to the student's self-assessment is of the utmost importance.

The third step is to explore the range of curricular opportunities available in the gerontology instructional program. A high percentage of students come to gerontology instruction with very vague and lightly held career goals. These change as the student becomes aware of the many possible job roles. The student should be encouraged to take courses in a variety of areas in order to learn about the wide range of possibilities and options.

The fourth step is to determine both short-term and long-term career goals. Many students have very limited employment goals. If they have been volunteers at the senior center, becoming a center staff member easily becomes their goal. If they worked part-time in a nursing home, becoming a local administrator is their aim. However, many students will have the opportunity to work at administrative and policy-making levels much higher than they initially anticipated, sometimes in government service, sometimes for national organizations, sometimes in national corporations. The limitations that students set on their own ambitions are frequently greater than necessary, and a sufficiently high employment goal, both initially and in the future, is very important.

The fifth step is to cultivate the skills necessary to acquire the desired position, a set of skills that is not always taught in gerontology programs. Included would be skills in developing a résumé, job-seeking approaches, and interviewing techniques; developing a network of contacts; and learning to describe clearly and concisely exactly what a gerontologist is and what the skills and abilities are that the job seeker has.

The final step looks to the future, to a career development process for the individual. The first job, although terribly important, is not the end of the career process; it should be carried forward by planning for future developments. Such developments frequently involve gaining recognition for the quality of work done, seeking additional responsibility, becoming involved in professional associations and community groups, and moving from one employer to another. The development of the long-range plan, and the modification of that plan when necessary, extends throughout the career; it is guided by knowing the desired goal that is being pursued by and maintaining perseverence in that quest. The goal will not necessarily be attained easily, but the opportunities exist for those persons who have the knowledge, skill, and commitment to pursue them.

Conclusion

Overall, nontraditional jobs in gerontology are the most difficult to describe, and they require careful career planning to access. Nevertheless, they are the forerunners of the diverse set of occupational roles that are developing outside the parameters of the traditional professional fields, and they may offer the greatest promise to the professional gerontologist. Students and others entering the field must be willing to accept the fact that today's employment roles are not protected by distinct job descriptions and civil service regulations. They are so new that they are fluid and flexible, an advantage for those professionals who have a clear understanding of their own skills and preferences, and who are willing to shape their roles and ultimately the whole field to gain a new understanding of what a gerontologist can be.

References

Bolton, C.R., & Scott, J.D. (1979). *Career planning in gerontology: A manual for guidance counselors.* Omaha: Gerontology Program, University of Nebraska.

Kahl, A. (1976). Jobs with service programs. *Occupational Outlook Quarterly, 20,* 13–29.

Kane, R.L., Solomon, D.H., Beck, J.C., Keeler, E., & Kane, R.A. (1980). *Geriatrics in the United States: Manpower projections and training considerations.* Santa Monica, Calif.: Rand Corporation.

National Institute on Adult Daycare. (1984). *Standards for adult day care.* Washington, D.C.: National Council on the Aging.

5
The History of Gerontology Instruction: Preparing Professionals for the Future of Gerontology

With the growth of the older population and the expansion of services and programs for older persons, an increasing number of professionals are employed in the field of aging. These persons currently number well over 1 million, many of whom have little or no gerontology training (Kahl 1976). The knowledge and skill of these individuals are crucial to the amount, effectiveness, efficiency, and appropriateness of services provided to older people. As the final recommendations from the 1981 White House Conference on Aging state, "The quality of educational services, and all other services available to older people, depends directly upon the quality of the personnel who provide them. All personnel involved in the delivery of such services should be required to have gerontological and/or geriatric training" (White House Conference on Aging 1982, 155).

To meet this need, gerontology instruction has developed rapidly in American colleges and universities during the past thirty years. Until very recently, the primary concern of the field was the need to expand instruction at all levels of higher education (Birren 1971; LaCharité and Associates 1977; Birren and Hirschfield 1979) and in as many professional areas as possible. Although a few observers concluded that "an appropriate number of gerontology programs and courses are now being offered" (Krishef 1982), the typical orientation was to exhort continued growth, for example in these recommendations from the White House Conference on Aging: "Therefore, we urge educational institutions at every level . . . to give high priority to the development and implementation of programs to educate and train on an ongoing basis senior adults, personnel serving the elderly, and the general public" (White House Conference on Aging 1982, 157).

It has not been clear, however, that current training is appropriately distributed, that is, proportional to the importance of the various service delivery fields and consistent with demands for personnel in these areas. This is necessary information because the educational preparation of personnel is generally the most significant variable in recruiting new persons to a field of service. Most persons working in the field of aging have not been educated as gerontologists but have obtained their training in another field. However, some content on aging is included in many other professional fields' training, from which a portion of the supply of personnel will be drawn.

As was noted previously, the future of gerontology as a profession will depend largely on the consumers—the growing population of older people. It is estimated that job opportunities will increase in a number of areas to meet the demands, and that those who have formal training in gerontology and are able to perform services specifically designed for the elderly will have an advantage. Thus, gerontology instruction also will be increasingly in demand.

Government Funding of Gerontology Instruction

Most gerontology instruction began after the passage of the Older Americans Act in 1965. Before that time individual courses were offered in various colleges and universities, but very few organized programs of instruction existed. Some institutions, such as the University of Michigan and the University of Chicago, had offered limited, community continuing education programs for older people, but no gerontology degrees or other credentials existed. If gerontology courses were offered at all, they were electives within one of the existing professions or disciplines.

Johnson (1980) has suggested that gerontology was conceived and born in academe, and developed in a manner similar to other disciplines or professions until 1965 when the popularization of the field altered its developmental process. The passage of the Older Americans Act as well as increased recognition of the growing population of older people has brought attention to related political issues, social concerns, and government programs. The Administration on Aging (AoA) has provided funds to support the development and operation of gerontology career preparation programs in American institutions of higher education.

The earliest career training programs emphasized graduate level training in areas that were not addressed by other federal programs, for instance, housing management, senior center direction, community planning, and administration of Area Agencies on Aging (Craig 1980). The first grants were made in 1966 to educational institutions, which agreed to offer basic course work in the psychobiological and socioeconomic aspects of aging and to place students in field practica.

Clark Tibbitts was the AoA staff member responsible for career training, and he encouraged the development of whole gerontology instructional programs, some of which led to separate degrees in gerontology, aging, or human development. The first of these degrees was offered at North Texas

State University in 1967; the University of South Florida created a degree one year later. AoA primarily funded master's degree instruction, while including some curriculum support. Although this effort was not entirely successful because of the different missions and priorities at the institutions involved, the degree programs that have been developed over the years have proved to be generally consistent (Peterson 1984).

The awarding of grants by AoA was a substantial motivator for many educational institutions. Between 1966 and 1984, AoA distributed nearly $80 million to 185 colleges, community colleges, and universities, as well as $15 million to 28 educational consortia (AoA n.d.). Although not all of these grants produced programs of instruction that continued after the completion of the applicable grant period, many did, and these programs comprose a substantial percentage of those that exist today. Funds were used to support not only educational institutions but also state agencies, Health, Education, and Welfare regional offices, and Area Agencies on Aging, so that short-term training could be made available in all parts of the nation.

AoA has continued to fund training programs over the past twenty years; however, the emphasis has changed as new legislation has been implemented. For instance, in 1973, funds were devoted to training new staff for the nutrition programs, Retired Senior Volunteer Programs, and Area Agencies on Aging. In 1975, emphasis was placed on developing institutionwide coordination, such as centers and institutes. At other points, priority was given to starting new programs in community colleges or undergraduate institutions. Later, the developing health care crisis led to the funding of long-term care gerontology centers at several institutions.

The Older Americans Act, therefore, can be given a great deal of credit for supporting and encouraging the development of gerontology instruction. However, a great opportunity was missed because the act included no requirement that employees of the Aging Network have some gerontology preparation before offering services to older people (Friedsam, in press). This decision substantially retarded the speed with which the field has been professionalized, but it was doubtless consistent with the preferences of the majority in the field at that time. The initial reason for this may have been that gerontology training programs were few and only a small number of people had such training. But although a tremendous opportunity to create and upgrade the field was lost, short-term training provisions for existing personnel were made widely available. Thus, many practitioners had the opportunity to gain at least an introductory knowledge of gerontology.

Continuing funding of career training also has been provided by the National Institute on Child Health and Human Development (NICHD), the National Institute on Aging (NIA), and the National Institute of Mental Health (NIMH). Many universities developed programs that acquired continuous funding, and a few became very visible, conducting comprehensive training programs within one of the disciplines or professions, or offering free-standing degrees in gerontology.

Most of this training was initially done at the master's degree level, but bachelor's and doctoral instruction also became popular. The most common approach was to create an organizational structure that was an institution-wide coordinating body, for example, a committee or center that would facilitate instruction across the entire institution. This allowed for drawing upon the resources of the various departments and developing a multidis-ciplinary instructional focus. The result was the development of several types of organizational structures, each with its own advantages and each being modified to fit the needs of the local institution. These structures included: intradepartmental programs, housed within a single discipline, usually psy-chology, sociology, or social work; committees on aging, cross-departmental groups of faculty who coordinate and advocate for programs of instruction; centers on aging, cross-departmental structures that typically have a physical place, some staff and budget, as well as responsibility for coordinating geron-tology instruction throughout the institution; and departments or schools of gerontology, with faculty lines, their own budgets, the authority to offer their own courses and in some cases to award gerontology degrees.

The appropriateness of awarding degrees in gerontology has been ques-tioned by some. Maddox (1978) sees gerontology as an adjunct to other pro-fessions or disciplines and assumes that having a degree in gerontology with-out extensive training in some other field will result in a disadvantaged posi-tion for the potential job seeker. However, Hirschfield and Peterson (1982) did not find this concern to be prevalent in a random sample of members of the Gerontological Society of America and of the Western Gerontological Society. Fifty-four percent of the respondents supported the idea of under-graduate degrees in gerontology; 82 percent supported the offering of master's degrees in this field; and 71 percent supported the development of doctoral degrees in gerontology. In general, persons who held master's or doctoral degrees were more favorably disposed than others to the idea of offering gerontology graduate degrees. Thus, the majority of people currently in the field, whether or not they have gerontology training, support the idea of gerontology degrees for those who are now entering the field.

The various structures noted earlier are important to delineate because of the differential control that they give to the gerontology faculty. The intrade-partmental programs and committees on aging provide relatively little con-trol over curriculum, students, and faculty, thus taking the determination of quality out the hands of the gerontology faculty. Departments or schools of gerontology have a great deal more control over these variables and thus are better able to assure that quality is achieved.

The expansion of instructional programs led to the creation of a national organization of gerontology instructional programs in 1974. Clark Tibbitts of the Administration on Aging took the lead in bringing together representatives of various instructional programs to discuss issues and plan for future developments. These meetings resulted in the creation of the Association for Gerontology in Higher Education (AGHE), an organization that currently has nearly three-hundred institutional members. AGHE conducts an annual conference on instruction, publishes a newsletter, offers technical assistance to new and developing instructional programs, conducts research on the extent and consistency of gerontology instruction, and represents the interest of many institutions in developing gerontology instruction.

Perceptions of Gerontology Education

The question now arises as to what extent this interest in and growth of gerontology instruction has continued. There has been no ongoing monitoring or counting of gerontology instructional programs. For this reason, data that would provide insight into the growth or decline of gerontology instruction in institutions of higher education have always been scarce. One measure used was the number of proposals received by federal agencies, but in years when little new federal money was available, or when restrictive priorities were placed on the funds, the number of submissions may have had little relation to the amount of interest. The result has been many unsubstantiated statements in the literature about the growth of gerontology instruction or the lack of it. Another result is that many uncoordinated studies have been conducted on separate parts of the field—on one profession, one state, one region, or one level of instruction—which have not been integrated into a comprehensive statement about trends in gerontology instruction in American higher education.

As the older population has grown and the number of service programs has expanded, many people have assumed that gerontology instruction has increased comparably. However, not every observer has shared this perception, and there has been some concern that gerontology instruction has not kept pace. A few examples should suffice. The first is from the National Institute on Aging: "To meet the needs of the elderly population, almost all health professionals and allied workers will require knowledge and skills with respect to aging and the aged. However, today relatively few have had opportunities to enhance their capabilities in these fields. To reduce the current gap and to ensure that future generations of health personnel have appropriate preparation is a critical and complex challenge" (NIA 1984, 13).

Likewise, the president of the National Association of Social Workers (NASW) recently indicated that social workers as a group do not have a strong awareness of the aged in society and called upon NASW and the Council on Social Work Education to exert "more leadership in order to assure that well-trained social workers [are] available to enter new and expanding markets" (Nelson and Schneider 1984, 1).

Similarly, the editor of *Gerontology and Geriatrics Education* recently indicated his perception that gerontology instruction was no longer developing: "I sense a lull in continued vigorous efforts to establish and maintain enlightened curricula in aging. There *are* notable exceptions. For all intents and purposes, however, there appears a silence which at times is deafening. Is this an inaccurate assessment? If not, where has everyone gone, and why?" (Levenson 1983, 1). Has gerontology instruction in colleges and universities continued to grow over the past twenty years? What do we know about its current trends?

The Association for Gerontology in Higher Education's *National Directory of Educational Programs in Gerontology* provides the only listing of gerontology instructional programs. The most recent edition (Lobenstine 1985) listed more than 250 community college, college, and university members, most of whom have formal programs of instruction sensitizing students to age-related change or preparing them to enter professional employment. At the present time, AGHE membership is nearly 300, suggesting that at least this many programs exist. Craig (1982) made a similar estimate (250–300 programs) by compiling a list of projects funded by AoA, NIMH, NIA, and the Health Resources and Services Administration (HRSA). He found, however, that only half the AGHE members were on his list.

However, the recent NIA (1984) *Report on Education and Training in Geriatrics and Gerontology* reviewed the data on gerontology instruction nationally and drew the conclusion that growth in the number of programs has been very limited: "While the precise number of institutions offering certificate and degree programs in aging is not known, it is estimated, on the basis of the membership of the Association of Gerontology in Higher Education, that the number approximates 100–125 institutions. In addition, about 100 other institutions offer coursework in this area. Information from applications to the Administration on Aging suggests an even higher estimate might be apropriate" (NIA 1984, 47).

This estimate of 200–225 institutions offering coursework in gerontology appears to be extremely low, particularly given previous studies which are described below. Although a number of these studies have collected data only by geographic region or have examined specific professions or content areas, individually they provide a good deal of insight into aspects of the field. However, collectively they do not result in a comprehensive understanding of the field. Still, it can be inferred from these data that the number of colleges and universities offering gerontology instruction is growing and has done so over the past twenty years. Several examples of this rapid growth can be extrapolated from these studies.

Previous Studies of Gerontology Instruction

In 1981, a survey of graduate schools of social work reached 64 of the 88 existing programs. It showed that course work in gerontology was available at 55 (86 percent) of the responding institutions (Nelson 1983). In 1983 a survey of the 94 existing programs resulted in a 100 percent response rate and indicated that 89 offered gerontology course work (95 percent) (Nelson and Schneider 1984). Also, the number of schools of social work offering graduate concentrations in gerontology increased from 23 in 1981 to 41 in 1983. Likewise, the American Personnel and Guidance Association reported that counselor education and counseling psychology departments offering course work in gerontology increased in number between the years 1975 and 1981 from 18 programs in 304 responding institutions (6 percent) (Salisbury 1975) to 114 (36 percent) in 314 (Myers 1983).

Doctoral programs that include gerontology courses show similar growth. In 1977 a survey of doctoral psychology programs showed that 67 of the 238 respondents (28 percent) offered course work in aging (Storandt 1977); the number had grown to 140 of 303 respondents (46 percent) by 1985 (American Psychological Association 1985).

Medical schools have also reacted recently to the need for increased instruction in geriatrics and gerontology. In 1980, approximately two-thirds of American medical schools offered instruction in geriatrics, and of these, one-half had been initiated since 1979 (Robbins, Vivell, and Beck 1982). By 1983, about 90 percent of the 100 responding medical schools indicated some activities in geriatric education (NIA 1984).

The number of dentistry schools that included some geriatric dentistry in the curriculum increased from 56 percent in 1974 to 100 percent in 1979 (Ettinger, Beck, and Jakobsen 1981) and remained at that level through 1984 (Moshman 1984). However, in 1979 the primary method of instruction consisted of occasional, supplemental lectures, with only 41 percent offering a series of lectures or a whole class on gerontology. By 1984, 58 percent of the 60 schools in the United States offered courses in geriatric dentistry.

Likewise, a few studies are available that indicate changes in the number of institutions offering instruction in gerontology in various geographic regions. For instance, California institutions of higher education were surveyed in 1975, and of 127 respondents, 50 (39 percent) offered courses in aging (California Office on Aging 1975). A 1981 survey, reaching 263 colleges and universities, reported 108 that offered courses in aging (41 percent) (California Council on Gerontology and Geriatrics 1981). Surveys of Michigan community colleges showed similar growth. In 1978, of 29 colleges, 11 (40 percent) offered courses in aging (Demko 1978), while in 1981, 14 of the 29 (48 percent) offered such courses (Demko 1981).

National surveys of all higher education institutions are very limited. Donahue (1960) in 1957 was able to identify 57 of the 2,500 institutions of higher education in the United States as offering credit courses in gerontology. The Gerontological Society (1968) conducted the first national survey of gerontology instruction in 1967. Of the 1,750 institutions surveyed, only 467 responded. Of these, 159 (34 percent) indicated that gerontology courses were currently being taught.

Nine years later, AGHE's first *National Directory of Educational Programs in Gerontology* (Sprouse 1976) was generated from a survey mailed to 3,000 colleges and universities. Of 1,276 responses, 607 institutions (48 percent) offered credit courses in gerontology (Bolton et al. 1978).

The data available from these surveys suggest that during the late 1970s and 1980s, the number of gerontology instructional programs has grown considerably.

AGHE-USC Study

In order to provide a more complete measure of this growth in gerontology instruction, the Association for Gerontology in Higher Education in cooperation with the Andrus Gerontology Center at the University of Southern California undertook a national survey on the extent of gerontology instruction. Funded by the Administration on Aging, the survey involved all American institutions of higher education. Questionnaires were mailed to the chief academic officer of all accredited community colleges, colleges, and universities in the country (Peterson, in press).

Questionnaires were mailed in early October of 1985, with a follow-up mailing early in December of 1985. The sampling unit was the campus; multiple campus institutions, such as the University of California, were treated as several separate campuses. Of 3,040 campuses that received questionnaires, 2,178, or 72 percent, had responded when the first data analysis was undertaken.

Of the 2,178 campuses from which responses were received, 1,105 indicated that at least one credit course in gerontology was offered regularly. This was the criterion used to categorize campuses as offering or not offering gerontology instruction. One credit course does not suggest much gerontology activity, but it does indicate whether aging content is regularly offered as a separate area of study. Using this criterion, approximately half of all responding campuses offered gerontology instruction. The mean number of courses per campus was 3.84, with most campuses offering 1 to 6 courses, but a few indicating more than 50 annually.

Larger institutions were much more likely to offer gerontology credit courses than were smaller institutions. Approximately 80 percent of the campuses with more than 10,000 students offered gerontology instruction, while only 41 percent of the campuses with fewer than 2,500 students did so. Likewise, larger institutions offered more courses on gerontology per campus; those with more than 10,000 students averaged 12.75 such courses, and campuses with fewer than 2,500 students offered 2.17.

A smaller number of campuses offered noncredit instruction, such as workshops, conferences, or occasional seminars. A total of 295 colleges and universities (about 16 percent of those responding to that question) offered noncredit instruction. Again, larger campuses were more likely to offer noncredit instruction, as were those that offered credit courses in gerontology. Since so few campuses offered noncredit courses, and since most offered credit courses at the same time, the data reported here will deal exclusively with credit instruction.

Public institutions were somewhat more likely to offer gerontology credit instruction than were private institutions. Fifty-six percent of the public institutions did so, compared with 46 percent of the private ones. Public institutions on average had a larger number of students and were likely to have developed gerontology instruction earlier than private institutions.

Institutions that offered higher degrees were also more likely to offer gerontology credit courses. Of colleges that offered only the associate degree, 36 percent offered gerontology courses; of those offering the bachelor's degree, 45 percent; of those offering master's degrees, 58 percent; and of those offering a doctorate, 78 percent.

Most campuses on which gerontology courses were offered were able to identify at least one "gerontology coordinating unit" at the institution. Whether this was a committee on aging, a gerontology center, an aging program, or some other unit was not studied at that point. Rather, the purpose was to discover whether there was some organizational focus for gerontology instruction, some place in the formal organizational structure where gerontology instruction was advocated, coordinated, and/or conducted.

Larger institutions were likely to have a greater number of gerontology coordinating units than were smaller ones. Thirty-three percent of the larger campuses (those with more than 10,000 students) had three or more coordinating units, while only 3 percent of small institutions (those with fewer than 2,500 students) did.

Several gerontology instructional programs were started before 1970, but many were initiated in the five years preceding the study. Fifty-nine of the campuses that offered gerontology instruction (7 percent) had begun offering those courses before 1970. Sixteen percent began between 1970 and 1974; 52 percent between 1975 and 1980; 23 percent between 1981 and 1985; and 2 percent were scheduled to be started in the near future.

Institutions that began offering gerontology instruction earlier were likely to offer more courses than were institutions that had recently begun gerontology instruction. Those that began offering such instruction before 1970 offered a mean of 16.7 credit courses, while those that started between 1981 and 1985 offered a mean of 3.6 courses. Again, larger institutions were more likely to have begun offering gerontology instruction early. Forty percent of the larger institutions (those with more than 10,000 students) began such instruction before 1975, while only 15 percent of the smaller institutions (those with fewer than 2,500 students) did.

This size distinction is significant because most American institutions of higher education are small. Fifty-eight percent of the institutions responding to this survey had fewer than 2,500 students. Approximately 500 of the 1,105 campuses offering gerontology instruction had fewer than 2,500 students. So, although the percentage of small campuses that offer gerontology instruction is lower than that of large campuses, much of the current instruction is done on small campuses. Small campuses also have great potential for future growth. Of the small campuses responding, 718 did not offer gerontology instruction, while only 57 of the large campuses did not. Thus, the first gerontology course remains to be developed in 59 percent of the small campuses that responded to the survey, plus an unknown percentage of nonrespondents.

Gerontology instruction was not evenly distributed on a geographic basis any more than it was on an institutional basis. In some states, most of the colleges and universities offered gerontology instruction, while in others relatively few of them had done so. For instance, more than two-thirds of all responding campuses in Connecticut, District of Columbia, Indiana, Rhode Island, Utah, and, Virginia offered gerontology instruction. On the other hand, fewer than one third of the responding campuses in Arkansas, New Hampshire, Montana, Puerto Rico, Vermont, and Wyoming offered gerontology instruction. Schools in rural states are least likely to have gerontology instruction, although present data do not shed any light on why this has occurred.

Gerontology instruction in American institutions of higher education has continued to grow over the past twenty years, both in the number of campuses offering credit courses and in the number of offerings per campus. From 57 campuses with gerontology instruction in 1957 (Donahue 1960), to 159 campuses identified as offering courses in 1967 (Gerontological Society of America 1968), to 607 in 1976 (Bolton et al. 1978), to the 1,105 identified in the 1985 AGHE/USC study, there has been a steady growth in the number of institutions involved.

At times federal agencies such as the Administration on Aging offered training grants, and there was a perceptible surge of development in gerontology instruction. However, the number of colleges and universities initiating gerontology credit courses has continued to increase regardless, indicating the growing recognition of this field of study and the willingness to organize courses dealing with aging content.

Much of the recent growth has been rather invisible—that is, it has not been accompanied by large federal grants, national program announcements, or huge commitments of resources. It is this lack of visibility that Levenson (1983) observed, but visible or not, the growth has continued as a grass roots response to the aging of society, indicating a recognition that gerontology is an important instructional area.

Growth has also occurred in the number of courses offered on each campus. Bolton et al. (1978) reported that the mean number of courses listed in the 1976 AGHE *National Directory of Educational Programs in Gerontology* was 3.24 for the 607 institutions offering gerontology instruction. The data from the AGHE-USC (1986) study indicated a mean of 3.84 courses per campus. Thus, while the number of institutions offering gerontology instruction had nearly doubled, the mean number of courses per campus also continued to increase.

Students' Interest in Gerontology

Although the increase in the extent of gerontology instruction has been verified, some ambiguity remains about students' interest in this area. The number of students enrolling in gerontology course work has increased rapidly over the past several years, partly because of the growth in the number of courses available. Institutions responding to the recent AGHE survey almost unanimously reported annual increases in total student enrollment in gerontology instruction. These are students who have sought out gerontology instruction and are pursuing gerontology as a career goal.

However, there is another, larger group of students whose interest in gerontology and geriatrics instruction is usually reported to be minimal. These are the students in related professional schools, such as those of medicine, dentistry, nursing, and so forth, who when offered the opportunity to gain some understanding of the processes of aging and the service delivery system that exists for older people are not likely to take advantage of it.

In this regard, LaCharité and Associates (1977) reported on a series of interviews with faculty and students in several professional schools of social work, nursing, medicine, public health, theology, education, law, communications, business administration, and architecture. They concluded that gerontology programs and courses were considered to be very low in status, importance, and availability by these groups. Michielutte and Diseker (1984/85) reported on the low interest of medical students in geriatrics as a specialty. Although knowledge of aging and older people increased over the course of the medical school experience, medical students reportedly exhibited little change in interest in working with older people. Likewise, Greenhill (1983) reported that a course of study in gerontology for undergraduate nursing students increased scores on an attitude measure but did not change the students' reported preference for a specialization. In terms of outcomes for those who do elect to take some gerontology courses, Belgrave, Lavin, Breslau, and Haug (1982) reported less stereotyping of the aged by medical students who were in a family practice specialty, chose medicine because of a service orientation, and preferred a primary care specialty. Health students interested in aging were likely to have had positive prior professional and personal contact with the elderly (Green, Keith, and Paulsen 1983).

Physician's assistants have been found to be more likely to be interested in geriatrics than are medical students (Michielutte and Diseker 1984/85). Social work students also seem generally more interested in gerontology preparation. When asked to identify their field of practice concentration, 6 percent of the social work students studied indicated aging/gerontological social work. This choice ranks fifth in order of preference behind mental health, health, family service, and child welfare, and ahead of such other choices as alcohol, drugs, community planning, corrections, groups services, industrial, and public assistance (Rubin 1984).

Conclusion

Much development must occur before all students in American institutions of higher education will have gerontology instruction available to them. However, the growth to date has been both substantial and consistent, and there is every reason to assume that it will continue in the future. From existing data, it can be suggested that this growth will occur in two areas. First, those colleges and universities that do not currently offer gerontology courses will initiate them. All large universities and most of those that offer graduate degrees will have gerontology courses within a few years, with the exception of a small number of technical schools. Smaller institutions, especially community colleges, will be slower to develop gerontology instruction, but most will include it by the turn of the century.

Second, gerontology instruction at larger institutions will continue to expand and differentiate. The number of courses per campus will continue to grow as additional departments initiate courses and others develop full programs of instruction. This will mean that students in many departments will have the opportunity to be exposed to gerontology instruction and to see its relationship to their academic major.

So where does all this leave us? Clearly, a great deal of progress has been made in making gerontology content available to college students but that much potential development remains to be accomplished. The coming years will see continuing expansion of gerontology instruction, and when it is available on every campus, it will provide the basis for eliminating the stereotypes and misinformation about aging and older people.

However, a goal of one gerontology course per campus is a modest and interim one. In the long run, gerontology instruction will need to be available to every student if societal attitudes and values are to be changed. Even greater expansion of course offerings will be needed if gerontological literacy is to be attained, and justice and dignity for older citizens is to be achieved.

Most of this new gerontology instruction has a liberal or scientific orientation since it is primarily taught at the undergraduate level. However, an increasing number of schools are creating and offering a sequence of gerontology courses that are professional in nature. This type of gerontology instruction will also increase in the future, and the number of persons prepared for roles in the field of aging will grow rapidly. In some parts of the country today, persons without gerontology training find it very difficult to acquire jobs in aging; this will become common across the nation in the future as new practitioners will be expected to have formal knowledge of gerontology before they are able to compete successfully for professional positions in service to older people.

References

Administration on Aging. (n.d.) Older Americans Act: Title IV training and multidisciplinary centers. Mimeo.

American Psychological Association. (1985). *A guide to doctoral study in the psychology of adult development and aging*. Washington, D.C.: American Psychological Association.

Belgrave, L.L., Lavin, B., Breslau, N., & Haug, M.R. (1982). Stereotyping of the aged by medical students. *Gerontology and Geriatrics Education, 3,* 37–44.

Birren, J.E. (1971). *Training in aging: Background and issues*. Washington, D.C.: White House Conference on Aging.

Birren, J.E., & Hirschfield, I.S. (1979). The emergence of gerontology in higher education in America. In H.L. Sterns, E.F. Ansello, B.M. Sprouse, & R. Layfield-Faux (Eds.), *Gerontology in higher education: Developing institutional and community strength*. Belmont, Calif.: Wadsworth.

Bolton, C.R., Eden, D.Z., Holcomb, J.R., & Sullivan, K.R. (1978). *Gerontology education in the United States: A research report*. Omaha: University of Nebraska.

California Council on Gerontology and Geriatrics. (1981). *Directory of gerontology and geriatrics education in California*. Los Angeles: Andrus Gerontology Center, University of Southern California.

California Office on Aging. (1975). *California higher education study for the aging*. Sacramento: California Office on Aging.

Craig, B. (1980). *A preliminary report on the development and implementation of a federal manpower policy for the field of aging*. Washington, D.C.: Administration on Aging, Office of Human Development Services, Department of Health and Human Services.

Craig, B.M. (1982). Weighing the issues and consequences of federal program termination: Administration on Aging support for career preparation. *Gerontology and Geriatrics Education, 3,* 129–137.

Demko, D.J. (1978). *In the service of older Americans: A survey of the activities of Michigan community colleges in the field of aging.* University Center, Mich.: Delta College.

Demko, D.J. (1981). *Policies and program in aging education: A survey of twenty-nine community colleges in Michigan.* University Center, Mich.: Delta College.

Donahue, W. (1960). Training in social gerontology. *Geriatrics, 15,* 501.

Ettinger, R., Beck, J.D., & Jacobsen, J. (1981). The development of teaching programs in geriatric dentistry in the United States from 1974 to 1979. *Special Care in Dentistry, 1,* 221–224.

Friedsam, H.J. (In press). Education in gerontology for service: Recurrent issues in the United States. *Educational Gerontology.*

Gerontological Society. (1968). *Final report: A survey of training needs and mechanisms in gerontology.* St. Louis, Mo.: Gerontological Society.

Green, S.K., Keith, K.J., & Paulsen, L.G. (1983). Medical students' attitudes towards the elderly. *Journal of the American Geriatrics Society, 31,* 305–309.

Greenhill, E.D. (1983). An evaluation of nursing students' attitudes and interest in working with older people. *Gerontology and Geriatrics Education, 4,* 83–88.

Hirschfield, I.S., & Peterson, D.A. (1982). The professionalization of gerontology. *The Gerontologist, 22,* 215–220.

Johnson, H.R. (1980). Introduction. In C. Tibbitts, H. Friedsam, P. Kerschner, G. Maddox, & H. McClusky. *Academic gerontology: Dilemmas of the 1980s.* Ann Arbor: University of Michigan Institute of Gerontology.

Kahl, A. (1976). Special jobs for special needs: An overview. *Occupational Outlook Quarterly, 20,* 2–5.

Krishef, C.H. (1982). Who works with the elderly? A study of personnel in gerontological settings. *Educational Gerontology, 8,* 259–268.

LaCharité, N., & Associates. (1977). *State of the art paper: Attitudes toward the elderly in professional education schools.* New York: Joseph A. Davis Consultants.

Levenson, A.J. (1983). Editorial: The calm before the storm in gerontologic and geriatric education. *Gerontology and Geriatrics Education, 4,* 1–2.

Lobenstine, J. (Ed.). (1985). *National directory of educational programs in gerontology.* Washington, D.C.: Association for Gerontology in Higher Education.

Maddox, G. (1978). How should gerontologists be educated? *Generations, 3,* 4–6.

Michielutte, R., & Diseker, R.A. (1984/85). Health care providers' perceptions of the elderly and level of interest in geriatrics as a specialty. *Gerontology and Geriatrics Education, 5,* 65–85.

Moshman Associates. (1984). *The status of geriatric dentistry in the undergraduate curriculum of the nation's dental schools: Summary report.* Bethesda, Md.: Moshman Associates.

Myers, J.E. (1983). Gerontological counseling training: The state of the art. *The Personnel and Guidance Journal, 61,* 398–401.

National Institute on Aging. (1984). *Report on education and training in geriatrics and gerontology.* Washington, D.C.: National Institute on Aging, Department of Health and Human Services.

Nelson, G.M. (1983). Gerontological social work: A curriculum review. *Educational Gerontology, 9,* 307–322.

Nelson, G.M., & Schneider, R.L. (1984). *The current status of gerontology in graduate work education.* New York: Council on Social Work Education.

Peterson, D.A. (1984). Are master's degrees in gerontology comparable? *The Gerontologist, 24,* 646–651.

Peterson, D.A. (In press). Extent of gerontology instruction in American institutions of higher education. *Educational Gerontology.*

Robbins, A.S., Vivell, S., & Beck, J.C. (1982). A study of geriatric training programs in the United States. *Journal of Medical Education, 57,* 79–86.

Rubin, A. (1984). *Statistics on social work education in the United States: 1983.* New York: Council on Social Work Education.

Salisbury, H. (1975). Counseling the elderly: A neglected area in counselor education. *Counselor Education and Supervision, 14,* 237–238.

Sprouse, B.M. (Ed.). (1976). *National directory of educational programs in gerontology,* First edition. Washington, D.C.: Department of Health, Education and Welfare, Office of Human Development, Administration on Aging.

Storandt, M. (1977). Graduate education in gerontological psychology: Results of a survey. *Educational Gerontology, 2,* 141–146.

White House Conference on Aging. (1982). *Final report, volume 3: Recommendations and post conference survey of delegates.* Washington, D.C.: White House Conference on Aging.

6

Knowledge and Skill Needed by Gerontology Professionals

G iven the growth of gerontology instruction and its expected continuation, it is important at this time to determine the goals and outcomes that should be expected. If gerontology is considered an area of liberal study, the outcomes can be expected to emphasize a generalized understanding of the processes of aging, the situations of contemporary older people, and the impact of aging on individuals, communities, and the general society. Likely to be added are more generic liberal arts outcomes, such as increasing the ability to think clearly and acquiring some awareness of the processes and results of empirical research. With liberal gerontology education as the objective, outcomes will vary substantially from one program to the next. Some programs will emphasize historical or philosophical understandings, some religious, some cultural or cross-cultural, some behavioral, and some physical. This diversity derives from the interests of the faculty and students, who are expected to pursue those topics that can provide some insight into appreciating and understanding the processes of aging.

If, on the other hand, gerontology is considered a professional area, then its instruction is the principal means of preparing professionals for employment, and the knowledge and skills that are gained take on an added importance. Professional gerontology instruction needs to be oriented to the background of the students, directed toward the types of employment roles available, and applied to conceptual and practical tasks that face planners, providers, and administrators of services to older people. Similarly, it needs to have some consistency from one institution to another so that employers can be assured that the graduates have similar skills and knowledge.

Curriculum Orientations

Determining the requisite knowledge and skills of a gerontology professional can be approached from several points of view. The most typical is for the faculty to identify the curricular outcomes of instructional programs. Many of these curricula are described in the literature, especially in the journal *Gerontology and Geriatrics Education.* For instance, Heisel (1981) and Ernst, Ernst, and Wilson (1982) have suggested an undergraduate gerontology curriculum; Romaniuk and Romaniuk (1984) have provided curriculum outcomes for mental health workers in aging; West (1981) has proposed a curriculum for nursing home administration; Kiyak, Small, and Allan (1981) have suggested environmental design content; Maxwell (1982) has offered geriatrics curricula for family practice residents; Segal (1983) has developed a dental geriatrics curriculum; Kolanowski (1983) has put forward a gerontology component for the nursing curriculum; and Warchawski (1983) has developed a curriculum for medical students. Other contributions toward program guidelines have come from a statewide task force on curriculum objectives for service providers in Virginia (Arling and Romaniuk 1980) and a model curriculum in health care developed at Ohio State University (McPherson, Liss, and McLeod 1983).

This faculty-generated approach to gerontology knowledge and skill was also undertaken by the Interuniversity Council on Social Gerontology, which met at the University of California at Berkeley in 1959. Fourteen Institute Fellows recommended a curriculum for social gerontology that has been followed widely in gerontology instructional programs in higher education. They developed syllabi in five areas—psychology, sociology, economics, social welfare, and an interdisciplinary approach to gerontology—which were published and distributed by the Division of Gerontology at the University of Michigan (Koller 1962). Although the specific readings and content are now dated, the disciplinary orientation, drawing from related behavioral and social sciences, has been accepted widely, as has the attempt to create new course content through an interdisciplinary seminar.

Although the Interuniversity Council curricula were widely distributed, no restrictions prevented faculty members or institutions from developing gerontology instruction in other forms. For example, in 1965 another development of gerontology curricula occurred when the U.S. Office on Aging (later to become the Administration on Aging) designed and published two-year curriculum titled *Training in Social Gerontology and Its Application* (Tibbitts 1967). This was designed to give students a basic knowledge of the field of aging, to help them apply this knowledge in the principal areas of employment, to enable them to gain experience through actual participation in programs or research, and to assist them in organizing and communicating this knowledge. Although still heavily focused on disciplinary content, this curriculum proposal was a significant step because it emphasized the application of gerontology knowledge in a variety of community-based services and programs and was designed to prepare students for employment in the newly developing field of aging.

Tibbitts' (1967) curriculum and the funding of gerontology instruction from the Administration on Aging served to expand gerontology instruction in American colleges and universities. In order to seek some consensus on a gerontology curriculum, the Association for Gerontology in Higher Education and the Gerontological Society of America undertook the Foundations for Gerontological Education Project (Johnson et al. 1980). In this project, the researchers solicited the views of a diverse group of knowledgeable persons about the content most appropriate for master's degree instruction in gerontology. Individuals knowledgeable in the field were identified, and a Delphi method was used to generate consensus regarding the topics of concern through a series of iterative questionnaires. One hundred persons recognized within the gerontological community for outstanding work in research, practice, or education were selected, including those from a wide range of disciplines and professions.

The Foundations Project addressed the issue of whether consensus existed on a common body of knowledge needed by all persons in the field of aging. At least 90 percent of the respondents indicated agreement with this concept. Participants were then asked to list topics and skills that should be included in the core content. Few of the skills were accepted by most of the respondents, but twelve of the content areas were considered sufficiently important to be included in the basic core of gerontology instruction by at least 70 percent of the participants. These areas included:

Psychology of aging

Health and aging

Biology of aging

Sensory change

Demography of aging

Sociology of aging

Environment and aging

Mental health and illness

Economics of aging

Attitudes toward aging

Public policy for the aged

Cognition and cognitive change

Despite these major sets of curricular recommendations for gerontology education, few studies have compared curricula at various levels (associate, bachelor's, master's, doctoral) in order to determine the consistency of program length, required courses, or fieldwork experience. In one study, Van Orman (1984) examined the curricula of 102 undergraduate programs listed in the 1982 AGHE *National Directory of Educational Programs in Gerontology* (Sullivan 1982). He asked program directors whether each of the forty-five content areas listed in the Foundations Project (Johnson et al. 1980) was included in their undergraduate curriculum. Sixty-six percent of the programs included at least 31 of the 45 topics, and 50 percent of the programs included at least 39 of the 45. This indicated a good deal of consistency in content currently offered at the undergraduate level.

In another study, Peterson (1984) compared the curricula of 19 gerontology master's degrees with the 12 highest-rated content areas reported in the Foundations Project. He found that 18 of the 19 programs included at least 11 of the 12 content areas. This suggested a significant level of consistency in the master's degree programs in gerontology. Further, it indicated that most of the degree programs in the country have accepted the content identified by the Foundations Project as a priority for their instructional programs.

The Foundations Project also attempted to identify skills that faculty perceived to be useful for various levels and types of students. There was much less agreement on this area than on necessary content. Only "understanding aging as a normal experience" and "respect for elderly, recognition of potential" received as much as 84 percent endorsement. As the authors of the study point out, these are really not skills but attitudes. The highest level of support, about 50 percent, for an actual skill was received by "ability to use research results," and 29 percent said that skills in conducting research were needed by all workers in the field of aging (Johnson et al. 1980).

The basic purpose of many meetings and some national organizations, such as the Association for Gerontology in Higher Education, is to enhance the quality of gerontology instruction. This is a valued outcome, but it is difficult to specify exactly what quality enhancement means. From the above discussion, it can be stated that while there is some agreement on the content that should be mastered by people who are preparing for employment in the field of aging, there is little agreement on the skills that they should acquire. This is understandable given the diversity of job roles in the field, but some additional consensus is needed on skills as well as on knowledge in order to ensure the quality of instruction for those who are seeking employment in applied services.

Davis School Outcomes

It was with this idea in mind that the faculty of the Leonard Davis School of Gerontology at the University of Southern California developed a set of instructional goals that all master's degree students are expected to attain (Davis School Faculty 1979). Although these goals or outcomes may not be completely applicable to other programs, they give a sense of the type of knowledge and skills that could be required of persons interested in securing employment in the field of aging.

In terms of *knowledge* outcomes, the student should have:

1. Factual knowledge of the processes of aging and the condition of older people in the contemporary United States
2. General and practical knowledge about subgroups of elderly
3. Knowledge of the structure and roles of national, state, and local programs for older people, and of local governments and organizations affecting public policy and programs for older people
4. Knowledge of the organization of the community, the resources for older people that are available, and the means of securing this information
5. Knowledge of him- or herself

In addition to this knowledge, the student should have *skills* in:

1. Applying scientific knowledge to an understanding of individual older people and to practice on their behalf
2. Assessing the present and future condition of individuals and groups of older people
3. Designing and implementing community-based programs
4. Managing and evaluating community-based programs
5. Promoting community change and advocacy
6. Using interpersonal communication and relations

Finally the student should have acquired *affective* and *philosophical* outcomes, such as:

1. A set of attitudes and beliefs that facilitate professional service and encourage continuing growth in members of the older population
2. A commitment to continuing his or her own personal and professional growth
3. A philosophy that guides professional practice and personal life

Professionals' and Employers' Views

Other sources of input on the skills and knowledge needed by a gerontologist can be used, for example, the perceptions of gerontology employers. A few studies have explored professionals' knowledge and skill needs from this point of view. Bolton, O'Neil, and Ball (1978) interviewed a number of persons in the Administration on Aging Network of community services, asking them to identify the skills and knowledge that were important in their jobs. They concluded that the most important work-related characteristics of professionals in gerontology cannot be gained in an educational setting. For direct service providers, the needed characteristics included the ability to relate to people, understanding of the problems and needs of the aging, knowledge of the physical changes that accompany aging, and communication skills with the elderly. For persons in administrative positions, skills in such areas as program planning, personnel management, budgeting, leadership, grant writing, research, and public relations were mentioned.

Van Orman (1984) compared the content of current undergraduate curricula with the content preferences of personnel in Area Agencies on Aging and state Offices on Aging and found that current employers desire persons with greater skills and less gerontology content knowledge. Ernst, Ernst, and Wilson (1982) reported that Area Agencies on Aging and nutrition project respondents included knowledge of gerontology as only one item in a list of twelve that were important for any prospective employee to have. Pratt and Simonson (1982) reported on prioritization of content in the area of medication and the aged as background to developing a course on that topic for nonpharmacy students.

Davis (1984) reported on a survey of 1,125 registered occupational therapists and 375 certified occupational therapy assistants. She had a 42 percent response rate and reported that the competencies perceived to be needed by the respondents included general gerontology, patient assessment, treatment approaches, and program management.

In general, when these researchers asked respondents to list what they considered to be necessary areas of skill and knowledge, gerontology content was a very minor part of the resulting list of topics. Generic skills such as an ability to plan and evaluate, interpersonal relationship skills, communication skills, and management skills were more frequently mentioned. In addition to skills, general characteristics such as a positive attitude toward older people, a desire to help, a commitment to service, and an appreciation for individual differences were often identified. All of these were worthy qualities, but they could result from many professional or disciplinary education programs and are not unique to gerontology.

Thus, gerontology employers have not yet grasped the idea of the unique integration of knowledge and skill that gerontology graduates are expected to have acquired. This combination allows them to modify more effectively and apply generic skills to a special audience, one that has many unique characteristics as well as multiple problems. The gerontology professional appreciates this uniqueness and is familiar with both traditional and innovative ways of providing service delivery.

Gerontology Alumni's Perceptions

Another approach to the development of a gerontology curriculum has been the exploration of the content deemed most important by graduates of gerontology master's degree programs. Peterson (1985) surveyed 438 graduates of fifteen gerontology master's degree programs to assess the didactic and experiential aspects that they in retrospect found were most helpful in their professional careers and to identify additional content or skills that they thought should be included in existing gerontology instruction.

Surprisingly, more than half of the respondents did not find professional skill development to be the principal orientation of the gerontology master's degree program that they had completed. Forty-three percent indicated that their program was principally job oriented, but 53 percent stated that the program emphasized a general understanding of aging rather than specifically preparing them for a professional employment role. This may well reflect the dichotomous orientation of gerontology education—with either an interest in social probelms and professional training or an emphasis on scientific understanding of the processes of aging. Although two-thirds of the programs did offer professional specializations in their master's curricula, more than half the students did not perceive their program to be oriented toward skill development.

Graduates of gerontology master's degree programs were overwhelmingly satisfied with the content of the instructional program from which they graduated. Seventy-three percent indicated that it prepared them for the job that they currently held, and 75 percent said that if they had it to do over again, they would choose a gerontology master's degree.

Interestingly, although most students desired a job-oriented degree program and did not find that their gerontology program fit this category, they still thought that the degree prepared them for their careers and concluded that they would pursue the degree again if given the opportunity. The perceived negative attributes of the gerontology degree involved concerns about the structure and legitimacy of the professional field of aging. Other degrees were seen as occasionally receiving preferential treatment in the employment market, and job opportunities were insufficiently attractive for some. Thus, the concern was not that gerontology curricula were inappropriately directed but that the employment field was not well developed and that job lines were somewhat ambiguous.

The graduates of the fifteen master's degree programs also were asked to list gerontological and other content that had been especially useful in their careers. The core disciplinary gerontology courses (biology, psychology, and sociology of aging) that are part of most instructional programs were the most frequently cited. It is not surprising that these three disciplinary areas were mentioned since they, respectively, were offered as separate, required courses by 79 percent, 74 percent, and 63 percent of the master's degree programs. These percentages suggest that basic knowledge in the core areas of gerontology is perceived as useful to persons employed in the field of aging and other professional areas.

Graduates were also asked to indicate the nongerontology courses that had proved to be the most useful in their careers. Courses in the area of management and administration were mentioned by 63 percent of the respondents. This response was given regardless of whether the graduate was currently in a job role that was characterized as management. Additional courses in psychology were listed by 18 percent, research methods (especially evaluation) were mentioned by 17 percent, and courses in counseling and interpersonal communication skills were identified by 17 percent.

When asked about areas that had not been included in their graduate program but that would have been useful in their careers, respondents again mentioned management-related courses most frequently (49 percent). Other topics that would have been useful included program planning and grantsmanship (18 percent), health care administration (13 percent), and counseling and communication skills (12 percent). Few respondents mentioned the need for additional theoretical courses or content related to understanding the aging process. Rather, the most frequently listed courses in this area were those involving skills.

When asked about the most useful part of the graduate program, respondents were most likely to identify the gerontology courses (44 percent) as most useful. However, 25 percent indicated that their internship, work in an agency or institution in the field of aging, was the most valuable. This is consistent with their preference for professional/practice courses. Respondents were asked to indicate whether the internship had been helpful in any of several ways. Since they could check multiple answers, the percentages total more than 100. The internship was seen by 65 percent of the respondents as a way to strengthen the skills that had been acquired through course work; 53 percent indicated that it was an opportunity to gain some direct experience in working with older persons; and 50 percent said that it provided professional contacts that would be useful in the future. It also had the benefit of providing a source of references for future job searches (27 percent), and it led to permanent employment for many graduates either in the specific internship organization or in other agencies (17 percent).

The conclusion can be drawn that the practical work experience of the internship was viewed by most of the alumni as a very important and useful

part of their graduate program. This is consistent with the vocational orientation of the alumni since the internship is a clear introduction to employment
and it sometimes led to jobs.

Conclusion

From the latter survey as well as the curricular recommendations of faculty, it
can be concluded that gerontology courses have been found to be valuable by
professionals currently employed in the field of aging. Likewise, internships
are overwhelmingly perceived to be useful, and they provide a number of substantial benefits to future professionals. Thus, educational preparation for
professional gerontology employment is strongly supported in the literature.

There are also suggestions from this literature that the knowledge and
skills that are currently being acquired by gerontology students are appropriate but in need of some modification, especially if the primary goal is preparation for employment. Many current students anticipate employment in the
field of aging and want educational preparation for that end. Like their pre-
decessors, many expect to assume administrative or program development
positions and could benefit from additional management knowledge and
skills in order to carry out these assignments successfully. Management, personnel, budgeting, and accounting skills were frequently mentioned, as were
grant writing, program planning, and evaluation. The data available do not
give any insight into the depth of knowledge and skill that is required or preferred, but it is doubtful that most alumni desired a full master's degree in
business or public administration. However, they did believe that they could
benefit from greater knowledge and skills in these areas.

Likewise, the need for enhanced interpersonal communication skills is
evident in the literature. Presumably, perceived needs in this area were
expressed by persons who did not have the opportunity to develop the personal interaction skills that would be useful when working with older individuals, their families, or small groups of clients. Individual and small group
skills are very useful for most professionals starting a gerontology career.

Gerontology education, although quite valuable and successful as it
stands, needs further refinement in order to include additional relevant skills.
Care must be taken, however, to avoid becoming so skills-oriented that the
curriculum loses its theoretical and content base, a base that allows professionals to accommodate successfully to the changes of the future. The
demands of the marketplace must be considered, but they must be balanced
against the insights of the faculty and the traditional curriculum to assure that
the instructional program is not only useful today, but that it will be valuable
in the future as well.

A balance between these two orientations will not be attained easily, but it is necessary if gerontology is to be accepted widely as a professional field. Faculty will need to assure not only that the scientific content is acquired but that the application of this content is clearly understood as well. Facts alone will be insufficient for meeting the challenges facing professional gerontologists; it is not sufficient to suggest that students should make their own translation to the field of practice. Instructional programs will need increasingly to involve faculty who have service provision experience as well as those with strong academic credentials in order to achieve the needed balance and assure that gerontology practitioners can work effectively for and with older people.

References

Arling, G., & Romaniuk, J.G. (1980). *Final report of the task force on gerontology in higher education.* Richmond, Va.: Virginia Commonwealth University.

Bolton, C., O'Neil, E., & Ball, J. (1978). *The determination of gerontology education appropriate to aging related occupational roles.* Omaha: University of Nebraska.

Davis, L. (1984). *Role of occupational therapy with the elderly (ROTE): AOTA member survey frequency distributions.* Washington, D.C.: American Occupational Therapy Association.

Davis School Faculty. (1979). Instructional outcomes of the Leonard Davis School of Gerontology, University of Southern California. Mimeo.

Ernst, M., Ernst, N., & Wilson, L. (1982). Developing an empirically grounded applied gerontology program. *Gerontology and Geriatrics Education, 2,* 183–189.

Heisel, M.A. (1981). *Guidelines for gerontology certificate/minor/concentration programs at the baccalaureate level.* New Brunswick, N.J.: Rutgers University Institute on Aging.

Johnson, H., Britton, J., Lang, C., Seltzer, M., Stanford, E., Yancik, R., Maklan, C., & Middleswarth, A. (1980). Foundations for gerontological education. *The Gerontologist, 20,* 1–61.

Kiyak, A., Small, R., & Allan, B. (1981). Teaching environmental design: Common needs of the elderly and persons with disabilities. *Gerontology and Geriatrics Education, 1,* 169–174.

Kolanowsi, A. (1983). Expansion of the gerontological component in a nursing curriculum. *Gerontology and Geriatrics Education, 3,* 207–211.

Koller, M.R. (1962). Recommended curricula in social gerontology. *Geriatrics, 17,* 260–264.

McPherson, C., Liss, L., & McLeod, D. (1983). Basic concepts for geriatrics/gerontology education. *Gerontology and Geriatrics Education, 4,* 11–21.

Maxwell, A. (1982). A geriatrics curriculum for the family practice residency. *Gerontology and Geriatrics Education, 2,* 213–217.

Peterson, D. (1984). Are master's degrees in gerontology comparable? *The Gerontologist, 24,* 646–651.

Peterson, D.A. (1985). Graduates' perceptions of gerontology master's degree curricula. *Gerontology and Geriatrics Education, 5,* 19–28.

Pratt, C., & Simonson, W. (1982). Pharmacists' and gerontologists' identification of content areas for coursework in geriatric pharmacy. *Gerontology and Geriatrics Education, 2,* 291–298.

Romaniuk, M., & Romaniuk, J.G. (1984). Curriculum content objectives for mental health service providers working with the aged. *Gerontology and Geriatrics Education, 4,* 57–69.

Segal, H. (1983). Establishing a dental geriatric curriculum. *Gerontology and Geriatrics Education, 3,* 297–305.

Sullivan, E. (Ed.). (1982). *National directory of educational programs in gerontology.* Washington, D.C.: Association for Gerontology in Higher Education.

Tibbitts, C. (1967). Social gerontology in education for the professions. In R.E. Kushner & M.E. Bunch (Eds.), *Graduate education in aging within the social sciences.* Ann Arbor: University of Michigan Division of Gerontology.

Van Orman, R. (March 1984). Bachelor's degree curricula in gerontology. Paper presented at Western Gerontological Society Meeting, Anaheim, California.

Warchawski, P. (1983). The introduction of medical students to gerontology and geriatrics. *Gerontology and Geriatrics Education, 3,* 227–231.

West, H.L. (1981). Curriculum for nursing home administration: A simulation methodology. *Gerontology and Geriatrics Education, 2,* 149–151.

7
Employment Experience of Gerontology Graduates

Many students who enroll in gerontology courses assume that work with the aging is an expanding field, implying a continuing growth in the number and availability of jobs. In general, this seems to be a valid assumption, as the existing and developing job roles described in chapters 3 and 4 underscore. The question is not whether jobs that relate to older people are becoming available, but rather what the employment experience is of students who have completed a college or university course of study in gerontology. Do they find jobs, and at what level?

Some difficulties arise in investigating this area. It is not easy to define who is a gerontologist or to determine equivalence in educational and experience levels. For instance, some students have taken only a course or two in gerontology, while others have completed a curriculum of study resulting in the award of a certificate, specialization, minor, or concentration in gerontology. Others have received an associate degree, a bachelor's degree, or a master's degree in aging. The backgrounds that these graduates bring to the employment field vary so substantially, and their view of themselves as gerontologists or as members of some other profession is so diverse that it is difficult to consider them as a single group of potential employees.

Likewise, it is difficult to specify what is meant by a job in the field of aging and to evaluate the appropriate employment level for a graduate of a gerontology program. Many jobs include some contacts with older people, for instance, those of police and firefighters, but holders of these jobs are generally not considered gerontologists. On the other hand, some administrators, program planners, and evaluators who work in the National Aging Network have relatively little contact with older people, yet they generally are considered to be employed in gerontology.

Studies of Gerontology Graduates

Two national studies have evaluated gerontology graduates' job experience, and several have dealt with graduates of individual colleges or universities.

Taken together, these studies provide a partial picture of what is occurring, but the surveys do not cover all types of gerontology students, at all levels, and in all areas of the nation. Therefore, we must be cautious and not draw conclusions that are too firm about what has happened to gerontology graduates.

Likewise, we must be cautious not to assume that the future will be exactly like the past. The latest study was completed in 1984, and most were conducted in the late 1970s. Changes in the economy, alterations in federal government funding priorities, and changes in local commitment to services for older people will all influence future gerontology employment.

The most comprehensive study of gerontology graduates, funded by the Administration on Aging, was carried out by Ketron, Inc. (1981). It involved a survey of students who had completed career training programs supported by the Administration on Aging at both undergraduate and graduate levels through 1978. The Ketron study reported that, of all students who had been enrolled in gerontology courses, 35 percent were employed in the field of aging, 42 percent were employed in other fields, 6 percent were seeking work, and 17 percent were continuing their education or were not in the labor market. For those who had received a degree in aging (both bachelor's and master's level students) 60 percent were employed in the field of aging, 14 percent were employed in other fields, 8 percent were students, 10 percent were seeking jobs, and 8 percent were outside the work force.

As has been noted, more limited studies also have been conducted that surveyed all of the graduates from separate instructional programs. For example, the three largest gerontology master's degree programs in the nation have conducted separate surveys of their graduates. North Texas State University reported that 81 percent of its graduates spent at least half of their time in service to the aging, 16 percent were employed in other areas, and 3 percent were furthering their education (Friedsam and Martin 1980). The University of South Florida reported that, of its employed graduates, 53 percent were employed in areas closely related to the field of aging, 39 percent worked in areas related to aging, and 8 percent were employed in areas not related to aging (Mangum and Rich 1980). The University of Southern California reported on the first two graduating classes of its master's degree program (Hartford 1980): 80 percent were employed in aging, 12 percent were in graduate school, 1 percent were unemployed, 3 percent were employed in other areas, and the status of 4 percent was unknown at that time.

Other studies of employment rates for master's degree students were reported by Wichita State University and the College of New Rochelle. In a 1982 report on gerontology master's degree graduates from Wichita State University, 92 percent were reported to have been employed part- or full-time in aging positions within six months of graduation, and 75 percent held such positions at the time of the survey, some having graduated more than four years previously (Hays 1982). Graduates from the College of New Rochelle's master's degree program were also surveyed (Doka and Smith-Fraser 1983). Although the response rate was only 33 percent, the findings indicated that most students had been employed before entering the program and continued to be afterwards. However, 56 percent of the respondents indicated that career mobility was enhanced because of the degree.

Two studies of the employment of gerontology bachelor's degree graduates have been reported. Wales and Oku (1980) reported on graduates of the University of Southern California program. Of the 61 percent responding, approximately 33 percent were employed in the field of aging, 33 percent were employed in other areas, and 33 percent were continuing their education. In a more comprehensive study, Fruit (1985) surveyed 303 graduates of bachelor's degree programs at twenty colleges and universities. She reported that 59 percent were employed full- or part-time in aging-related positions, and 27 percent were employed in other types of jobs. Persons in aging-related jobs were employed in residential, business, government, health-related, social service, education, and recreation areas. They reported their major responsibilities to be administration (37 percent), direct services (25 percent), health services (12 percent), planning (9 percent), education (4 percent), and other (13 percent).

The Ketron data suggested that several factors were helpful to graduates in obtaining jobs in aging. Any kind of previous work experience was important, with 80 percent of those graduates with full-time experience securing employment in aging, as compared with 67 percent who had not had previous employment. Work experience in aging was also helpful in gaining employment in the field. Seventy-eight percent of graduates who had worked in aging returned to jobs in the area, whereas only 40 percent of those with no work experience in aging went into the field. Volunteer experience was also likely to lead to employment, as was a field placement in aging. Males were more likely to find jobs than females, as were whites when compared with members of minority groups (Ketron 1981). The question thus arises as to how reflective these differences are in terms of the characteristics of gerontology graduates in general.

Graduates of Gerontology Master's Degree Programs

Peterson (1985) surveyed 438 graduates of fifteen master's degree programs in gerontology. The vast majority of the respondents were female (73 percent), Caucasian (93 percent), and at least thirty years of age (70 percent). Most (72 percent) had been employed before entering the graduate program, 38 percent full- or part-time in the field of aging, and nearly two-fifths of them had some volunteer experience. Most of the graduates entered the master's degree program in order to secure or continue employment in the field of aging.

Fifty-nine percent of the respondents indicated that they were currently employed full-time in the field of aging, and 6 percent were employed in aging part-time. Seventeen percent reported being employed full-time in some other field, and 3 percent were employed part-time in a nonaging field. The remainder were out of the work force, retired, or indicated some other situation. It appears that most graduates sought a position in the field of aging, but those who were not able to find full-time employment in aging migrated to other fields several months after graduation. As indicated in the Ketron study, persons who were employed full- or part-time in aging before entering the master's degree program were more likely than others to have secured employment in the field of aging after completing the degree.

Current employment varied somewhat according to educational specialization within the master's degree program. Those who identified themselves as completing a health/long-term care specialization or an administrative specialization were the most likely to have found full-time employment in aging (79 percent and 72 percent, respectively).

In general, persons completing a particular specialization were likely to identify that specialization area as the one in which their current job responsibilities were concentrated. For instance, 67 percent of those who specialized in administration/management reported administration to be their primary responsibility. Fifty percent of those who specialized in direct service reported it as their major area of responsibility, while 23 percent reported administration as their primary role. Fifty-five percent of those who specialized in education reported it as their major role. Only 19 percent of those who identified health/long-term care as their specialization reported that their principal role was in the same area. However, 55 percent of the health specialists indicated administration as their major role, so definitions rather than movement away from the field probably explain this low figure.

Nineteen percent (85) of the graduates indicated that they were currently employed in an agency or organization that was part of the National Aging Network, while 61 percent indicated that they were not. Those persons employed in the network were likely to indicate their primary responsibilities as administration (53 percent), direct service (20 percent), program planning and evaluation (14 percent), or other (13 percent).

Graduates were employed in a wide variety of organizations. The largest percentage worked in homes for the aged, while government agencies, nursing homes, educational institutions, and proprietary settings were identified by many graduates. Graduates of North Texas State University (NTSU) comprosed a large proportion of the respondents (29 percent). Since that program emphasizes long-term care and administration of homes for the aged, the number of persons working in the area is somewhat overemphasized.

Of the 393 persons who provided their current job titles, 66 percent held jobs that were categorized as administrative in nature. These jobs included such titles as administrator, program developer, policy analyst, personnel manager, consultant, nursing home owner, and intern. The other 34 percent of respondents had such titles as instructor, nurse, allied health professional, counselor, direct service personnel, minister, social worker, researcher, gerontologist, sales personnel, paralegal, volunteer, and technician. These job titles were grouped into five role categories:

13 percent of the respondents were in public affairs–social science roles

6 percent were in educational roles

6 percent were in nonprofessional positions

6 percent were in health-related positions

3 percent were in research

Again, NTSU graduates were disproportionately represented in the administrative category. Eighty-five percent of NTSU graduates listed their jobs as administrative, while 58 percent of all other respondents gave administrative titles.

Men were somewhat more likely to have administrative titles than were women (74 percent to 63 percent), and administrators were likely to have higher salaries than nonadministrators. The mean annual salary for administrators was $25,446, while the nonadministrators had a mean annual salary of $20,350. Men generally had higher salaries than women. In administrative positions, men had an annual mean of $31,368, while women received $22,485. In nonadministrative positions, men averaged $23,850, while women earned $19,180.

The length of time since graduation was clearly associated with administrative status. The greater the number of years since graduation, the more likely the individual was to have an administrative title. This results primarily from the NTSU graduates' composing the majority of the early graduates, but it does reflect the fact that some gerontology graduates move to administrative positions.

From anecdotal evidence, it had been presumed that professionals in the field of aging frequently entered the work force as direct service personnel and eventually were promoted to supervisory or administrative positions. This assumption was not completely supported by the data from this survey. There was a tendency for graduates to move from a variety of roles to ones that could be considered administrative or management in orientation: however, most of the graduates acquired administrative roles in their first jobs and remained in this type of position, whether or not their titles changed.

As would be expected, graduates who had specialized in administration in their master's degree program were more likely to have acquired a position in this area initially. Graduates with specializations in direct service, education, and program planning were most likely to have moved into administrative roles after an initial nonadministrative position.

A previous professional degree, such as one in nursing, social work, education, law, management, occupational or physical therapy, public administration, or divinity, did not seem to be an advantage in job seeking. Those with a previous professional degree were no more likely to be employed in general or to be employed specifically in the field of aging than those without previous degrees. Persons with a previous professional degree were more likely to have held previous full-time employment but less likely to report increased responsibility since completing their graduate gerontology degree.

A concern of some potential gerontology students is whether employment opportunities in the field of aging provide future growth challenges. Respondents in the survey were therefore asked whether they had experienced increasing responsibilities in their jobs. Eighty-six percent of those responding indicated that they had, and 89 percent of those employed full-time in the field of again perceived this positive movement. Of those persons who identified administration/management as their primary role, 91 percent said that they had experienced increasing responsibility.

Methods of securing employment in aging varied widely among the respondents. No single means was found effective by many of the graduates.

14 percent found jobs through newspaer advertisements

11 percent received help from a mentor

10 percent found employment through their field placements

9 percent were assisted by a gerontology faculty member

4 percent found jobs through a professional association

4 percent, through alumni of the program

4 percent, through a volunteer role

3 percent through a placement service

41 percent checked the "other" category, indicating a wide range of contacts and events

This indicates that no single approach to job seeking has proved successful for most degree graduates.

A typical concern for persons considering a gerontology degree is whether it is a "salable" credential in the job market. Seventy-one percent of respondents indicated that their current job had been acquired because they had a gerontology master's degree. Of those currently employed full-time in the field of aging, 82 percent indicated that they had acquired their jobs because of the gerontology degree. Likewise, 79 percent of the respondents indicated that the gerontology degree had been valuable in their career. Of those persons employed full-time in aging, 90 percent said that the degree had been valuable.

Most of the graduates (78 percent) reported that the gerontology master's degree had prepared them for their career to date, although a total of 58 percent also said that some other degree might have been just as valuable. Three-quarters of the respondents said that when assessing their gerontology experience, with hindsight, they would choose a graduate gerontology program again. Of those employed full-time in aging, 82 percent stated that they would choose gerontology again.

Comparative Success of Gerontology Employment

There has been no direct attempt to compare gerontology degree graduates' success in finding employment with that of other departments' graduates. Kahl (1983) has suggested an indirect approach. Data from the National Center on Educational Statistics (NCES) can be used to explore the extent to which graduates of different fields secure "appropriate" employment—that is, employment that requires a college degree. This type of employment included positions that are listed as professional, technical, managerial, administrative, and nonretail sales; whereas occupations that did not require a college degree included retail sales, clerical, craft, operative, laborer, service, and farm groups.

Kahl (1983) reported that students trained in various fields differed significantly in the percentage of those employed in jobs requiring a college education. At the top of the list were nursing, accounting, and engineering, which placed 85–95 percent of their graduates in such "appropriate" positions. At the other end of the spectrum were sociology, social work, psychology, history, and fine and applied arts, which placed approximately half of their graduates in jobs that required a college education.

Although questions posed by Fruit (1985) to gerontology bachelor's degree graduates were not the same as those used in the NCES study, respondents were asked to list specific job titles. Of the 216 who did, 200 (or 93 percent of them were clearly "appropriately" placed—that is, not in sales, clerical, craft, operative, laborer, or farm occupations. Gerontology bachelor's degree graduates therefore appear to have been substantially more successful at securing "appropriate" levels of jobs than those from the social sciences, humanities, and arts.

The NCES data (Kahl 1983) indicated that 93 percent of master's degree recipients nationally were employed in an "appropriate" position within six months of graduation. Of the employed gerontology master's degree recipients in Peterson's (1985) study, 94 percent were working in professional level positions, which can be considered to be at an "appropriate" level.

The appropriateness of the job is important because it is the base from which career advancement occurs. If graduates do not initially achieve this job placement and must seek advancement from clerical or service positions to professional status, then progress up the career ladder will be extremely slow and difficult. Since most gerontology graduates seem to acquire professional level positions, they have gained that first level of job placement and are well situated to achieve increases in responsibility, status, and income.

Conclusion

The data from these studies indicate that persons completing gerontology master's degrees are faring reasonably well in the job market. Previous employment, academic specialization completed, previous professional degree, and program size did not have as great an impact as might have been expected. It appears that having the gerontology master's degree is the primary variable.

These data help to answer questions about the job experience of gerontology master's degree graduates, but they still need interpretation. Is 60 percent, 65 percent, 80 percent, or 84 percent employment in aging good enough? There are no norms against which to compare these data, and subjective expectations vary from one person to another. However, for a new field with only a few universities and colleges offering the degree, no current licensure or certification of graduates, in a difficult economic climate, and with a trend away from the growth of human service programs, it would appear that gerontology graduates have done very well in the job market. The master's degree programs have been successful in their mission of preparing personnel to serve older persons and their families in a variety of organizational settings. The graduates are overwhelmingly satisfied with the results of their education, they are currently employed in the field of aging, and they appear to be prepared to remain there gaining the benefits of their education for many years to come.

The data and anecdotal experience suggest that securing employment in the field of aging occurs in a variety of ways. Some graduates find jobs through their faculty advisors or program placement services. Most however, find them through some less expected means, for instance, through newspaper ads, by hearing about them from friends, or through their field placements. Coyle (1985) has pointed out that it is useful for those interested in gerontology employment to market themselves wisely, that is, to identify the skills that they have acquired and find job markets where these will be perceived as valuable.

Graduates generally are satisfied with their degrees but often must take advantage of personal and faculty networks in order to be sure of finding a job. As Sinick and McKibbin (n.d.) point out, there is a major need for some kind of a national placement service in gerontology. Although attempted for short periods in the past, these services have not proved effective because of the variety in types of jobs, levels of positions, and local hiring practices of many organizations. Until a state or national service exists, graduates of gerontology programs will need to create networks and seek jobs from a variety of sources.

What is the future prospect for employment of gerontologists? It would appear to be bright. The growth of the older population will continue, the demand for services will rise, and the quality of life for most Americans will continue to increase. Government funding is likely to remain strong, and the ability of older people to pay, either personally or through third-party arrangements, will increase.

The health field holds high promise for gerontologists seeking employment. Agencies that provide home-delivered health services are springing up in many communities, some supported by federal and state funds and others depending upon private philanthropy or fees paid by the older consumer. These organizations provide new and improved service approaches, and they will need not only large numbers of employees, but personnel who are able to conceive new ways of responding to needs rather than relying on the service delivery models of the past.

Similarly, growth can be expected in the private sector, as corporations and businesses expand their marketing of goods to the older consumer. Marketing to older people is becoming more common, and the future will see most producers of goods and services join the travel agencies, restaurants, drug manufacturers, and hospitals in overt competition for the older person's discretionary income. This will bring about job roles for those who can recognize unmet needs and can creatively design products and services specifically for the older consumer.

In competing for these new occupational roles, professional gerontologists will need to be innovative in identifying opportunities and presenting themselves in ways that are appealing to employers. This will require a clear understanding not only of the older population but also of the skills that the professional has and the ways that he or she can aid both the employer and the older person. Flexibility and initiative will be needed, and if handled appropriately, the employment opportunities for gerontologists in the future should be even more diverse, challenging, and rewarding than they have been in the past.

References

Coyle, J.M. (1985). Entrepreneurial gerontology: Creative marketing of gerontological skills. *Educational Gerontology, 11,* 161–167.

Doka, K.J., & Smith-Fraser, D. (1983). Master's practitioners in gerontology: A preliminary report. Paper presented at the New York State Association of Gerontology Educators, New York City.

Friedsam, H.J., & Martin, C.A. (1980). An applied program in social gerontology: A report on ten years' experience. *The Gerontologist, 20,* 514–518.

Fruit, D. (1985). Are graduates of bachelor's degree programs in gerontology employed? A report of a national survey. *Educational Gerontology, 11,* 237–245.

Hartford, M.E. (1980). Study of the vocational interests of the first two master's degree classes of the Leonard Davis School 1975–1976. *The Gerontologist, 20,* 526–533.

Hays, W.C. (1982). Employment experience of Wichita State University gerontology graduates. Paper presented at the Thirty-fifth Annual Scientific Meeting of the Gerontological Society of America, Boston.

Kahl, A. (1983). The job outlook for college graduates: What does it mean for gerontology? Mimeo.

Ketron, Inc. (1981). *Evaluation of the Title IV-A career training program in aging.* Washington, D.C.: Ketron, Inc.

Mangum, W.P., & Rich, T.A. (1980). Ten years of career training in gerontology: The University of South Florida experience. *The Gerontologist, 20,* 519–525.

Peterson, D.A. (1985). Employment experience of gerontology master's degree graduates. *The Gerontologist, 25,* 514–519.

Sinick, D., & McKibbin, G.B. (n.d.). *Linking gerontology jobs and workers.* San Francisco: Western Gerontological Society.

Wales, J.B., & Oku, L. (1980). Career patterns of graduates from a multidisciplinary undergraduate program in gerontology. Unpublished report. Los Angeles: Andrus Gerontology Center, University of Southern California.

8
Current Gerontology Professionals and Their Continuing Development

Although gerontology instruction is on the rise, opening many opportunities for future gerontologists, an equally vital need remains for providing educational opportunities to those currently working in the field who did not have the benefit of such instruction. As was pointed out in previous chapters, professionals working in aging enter the field in a variety of ways—through a related profession, a volunteer role, promotion from clerical or support service, as well as from a gerontology instruction program at a college or university. The implication of this open entry system is that people working in the field have relatively little formal education regarding aging or older people. This is a major concern, since many of these professionals may hold the same inaccurate stereotypes about aging and older people that are prevalent in society generally. These would include negative attitudes toward aging, negative expectations of the potential of older people, lack of understanding of the multiple and interrelated problems that affect many older people, and no familiarity with the service delivery systems that have been created to serve older adults. Thus, continuing education for those already in the field of gerontology is vital to upgrading the field and to increasing the professionalism of its staff.

Kahl (1976) estimated that in 1976 more than 1 million people worked in areas associated with the field of aging. This number has certainly increased greatly since that time and now probably approaches 1.5 million. Of these, approximately three-quarters are employed in nursing homes, with nurses' aides and orderlies being the largest group. This does not mean that no professional level positions exist, but only that in gerontology, as in other fields, most of the jobs are at a lower level of education and salary. There is no general agreement on which job roles should be considered to be within the field of aging because of the different definitions used and the rapid growth of some sectors, such a nursing homes. Many professionals relate to older people only peripherally as part of their service to people of all ages, while others in the same profession may concentrate their service on older people. For example, more than 12 percent of the members of the American Home Ecoomics Association work primarily with persons age sixty and over (Fanslow et al. 1979).

Few surveys have provided data on the educational and other demographic characteristics of employees in the field of aging. Such studies have typically dealt with only a small sample, generally in one geographic area, but they do provide some insight into the backgrounds of current practitioners working with the aged. Hirschfield's (1979) survey of a random sample of the members of the Gerontological Society of America and the Western Gerontological Society indicated that 61 percent of the respondents were female, 86 percent were Caucasian, and more than 70 percent had a master's or higher degree. Members of the GSA sections on clinical medicine and biological science were more likely to be male and to have doctoral degrees than those in other sections.

Fleming, Green, and Rich (1982) reported that of 736 personnel working in Florida Area Agencies on Aging, 81 percent were female, 50 percent had some college education, 13 percent had an undergraduate degree, and 14 percent had a graduate degree. The sample included clerical and support staff as well as those involved in administration and direct service provision. Males were overrepresented in the administrative category, and persons in direct service had achieved the highest level of formal education. Krishef (1982) reported a somewhat more encouraging situation. He surveyed a stratified sample of Florida's Area Agencies on Aging, community mental health centers, and multipurpose senior centers and reported on the characteristics of professional staff. Seventy-five percent of the respondents were female; 66 percent had a bachelor's degree, and 35 percent held a master's degree. Sixty-three percent had worked in the field of aging two years or fewer. Klegon (1980) reported a survey of agencies serving older people in a nine-county area of Ohio. Of the 315 responding professional staff, 35 percent had a bachelor's degree. Personnel in agencies exclusively serving the aging had less formal education than did others.

The characteristics of persons employed in the National Aging Network have been collected in a national data base by the National Association of State Units on Aging (NASUA) and the National Association of Area Agencies on Aging (N4A) (National Data Base on Aging 1986). Of the 2,155 staff members of thirty-nine state units on aging for which data were available, more than two-thirds were female, 18 percent were minority group members, and 8 percent were over the age of sixty. The median number of staff for a state agency on aging was 25, of whom 24 were full-time employees. Nearly 53 percent were employed in professional positions. Of the 39 directors of the state units on aging, 5 had received an academic specialization in gerontology during their college preparation.

Data were also provided on 121 Area Agencies on Aging (of the 666 currently in existence). A total of 2,238 persons were employed in these Area

Agencies, with 77 percent being female, 15 percent minority, and 25 percent over age sixty. The median number of staff per agency was 9.5, with 7 of these holding full-time positions. Only 37 percent of the employees were in professional/managerial positions, with 14 percent being clerical and 49 percent being "other nonclerical." Seventeen percent had completed a specialization in gerontology during their college preparation. Nearly half the directors of both state and Area Agencies held a master's or higher degree. Data were not provided on the educational level of staff (National Data Base on Aging 1986).

To the extent that these descriptions of persons currently employed in the field of aging can be generalized, they suggest that gerontology practitioners have fairly low levels of formal education and relatively little formal gerontology preparation for their professional roles. Certainly this perception fits with the numerous examples that could be provided of middle-aged women returning to work and finding employment in this field, of retirees (both men and women) who have accepted part-time jobs in aging programs, and of persons who have worked their way up in social or health service organizations from clerical and support positions to quasi-administrative positions and full professional status.

Gerontology Education Background of Current Employees

The few studies that have examined the backgrounds of people in the field of aging indicate that approximately 10 percent have had some gerontology course work during their educational preparation. Jackson (cited in Strasburg 1984) reported that only 10 percent of practicing physical therapists had any preparation in gerontology, most of it from workshops and conferences they had attended after beginning work in the field. Similarly, Simonson (1981), in a survey of currently practicing pharmacists, asked to what extent their formal training prepared them to understand medication use and misuse by the elderly and found that 81 percent of the respondents were prepared only slightly or not at all to handle this issue.

Klegon (1980) reported that for an Ohio sample of persons employed in agencies serving the elderly, only one-quarter indicated any training in aging prior to beginning work in the field, only 9 percent had enrolled in gerontology courses since obtaining their first job in the field of aging, and only one-third had even taken a noncredit workshop since beginning work in the field. Johnson and Kim (1984) surveyed Master of Social Work graduates of two social work schools who were currently employed in the social service field. They reported that fewer than 10 percent had completed at least one course or workshop in aging during their formal training. Furthermore, fewer than one-third had read an article or book on aging in the past year. Krishef

(1982), on the other hand, reported that of his Florida sample, 70 percent had taken at least two courses in aging, and among those with a master's degree, gerontology was the most frequently indicated major. Eighty percent of the persons surveyed had also received some in-service training in gerontology.

Although the available data are not very complete on the background of current gerontology practitioners, it would appear that changes are occurring. In the past, most of the personnel accepted their first job in aging with little or no formal preparation. They learned about the field on the job, through occasional workshops offered by colleges and universities or government agencies, or by individual reading and watching media. On the other hand, some may have learned relatively little academic gerontology through these processes but managed to carry out the job responsibilities anyway. More recently, as instructional programs have become common, persons entering the field are likely to have some, although not much, academic gerontology background.

Current Opportunities for Professional Development

Professionals in the field of aging are now discovering a number of opportunities for increasing their knowledge: workshops, conferences, publications, and media presentations. The number of these options has grown rapidly, as many colleges, universities, and other organizations have expanded their offerings and focused their content on more specific areas in the field.

One development that facilitated the growth of continuing gerontology education was in the early implementation of faculty training. Although most faculty, like most service providers, had little formal preparation in gerontology, an early activity in several universities was to offer faculty development workshops or programs to assist current faculty in identifying major research, concepts, and materials that could direct the modification of courses and the creation of practitioner training in gerontology. For example, the Interuniversity Council on Social Gerontology, briefly described in chapter 2, and other faculty development programs at the University of Michigan (Peterson, Donahue, and Tibbitts 1972) and at the extensive Summer Institute at the University of Southern California have provided such exposure to many faculty members.

Further, federal agencies have consistently devoted resources to the upgrading of staff who are employed in agencies carrying out their mandated programs. For instance, the Administration on Aging has funneled a portion of the available training funds to state units on aging, which coordinate or contract with other agencies or institutions to conduct training for staff in the National Aging Network. Also, Title XX of the Social Security Act for a number of years provided training funds for practitioners in the social service network, and financial support from the Administration on Aging (AoA), National Institute on Aging (NIA), National Institute of Mental Health (NIMH), and other government agencies has led to what Tibbitts called the "short term training industry" (Tibbitts 1980). At one time this industry was primarily the domain of higher education training programs, but as federal funds were made available to other providers, programs began to be sponsored by professional and trade associations, nonprofit organizations, and private enterpreneurs. As long as the employment of persons in aging services with little or no background in gerontology continues, this industry will flourish (Friedsam, in press).

National associations have also taken leadership roles in the continuing education of staff in the field of aging. The National Association of State Units in Aging (NASUA) and the National Association of Area Agencies on Aging (N4A) have developed and regularly offered training programs for employees of their membership agencies. Organizations such as the American Society on Aging (formerly the Western Gerontological Society) have expanded their training efforts to all parts of the nation, and many hospitals and medical centers have begun offering short courses and workshops for their staff and others.

In the health field, continuing education is required to maintain licensure for nursing home administrators, nurses, social workers, and others. This situation has created many one- or two-day workshops that meet the licensing requirements and update people on new developments in the field. The American College of Nursing Home Administrators, the American Health Care Association, the American Association of Homes for the Aging, the National Council on the Aging, and many state professional associations have entered this area.

Required continuing professional education poses many problems. Some practitioners do not feel the need to attend class sessions and prefer independent reading and study. Others find it difficult to make the time to be away from the job, so they enroll in a course that is nearby or convenient rather than one that would be of the most value. Instructional providers offer the courses that will draw the largest group of professionals in order to cover the costs of instruction. Thus, a better system is needed to help professionals identify their knowledge and skill weaknesses and to help them continue their professional development.

Current Gerontology Continuing Education Offerings

The content of continuing education programs in gerontology varies greatly. In the past, many of these programs focused on academic gerontology, a condensation of the course work offered in college and university curricula, dealing with the biological, psychological, and social aspects of aging. As larger numbers of people completed this overview, workshop emphasis changed to new legislation, program requirements, and new service delivery approaches (for example, case management). Most recently, workshops on Alzheimer's disease and related disorders have become common, as have those on oral history, microcomputers, communication techniques, and changes in government regulations.

There are relatively few data to draw upon to determine the demand for continuing gerontology education outside that required by licensure. Programs continue to multiply so the demand must exist, but the literature provides little confirmation of this. Cyr and White (1982) reported that thirty-eight states required an annual average of twenty-three contact hours of continuing education for the renewal of nursing home administrator licenses. In this study, administrators, both in states that had an annual continuing education requirement and in ones that did not, reported an annual average of twenty-eight contact hours. The course subjects most frequently selected were administration, laws and regulations, psychology/social aspects, medical care, and community relations. Additional topics reported as essential included personnel management, patient care, and departmental supervision. Of 25,000 licensed administrators, approximately 2,153 had earned postemployment academic degrees, primarily in the field of business administration.

Persons in nonadministrative positions are more likely to see other types of content as preferable to management instruction. For instance, in a statewide needs assessment of persons in the Florida Aging Network, Fleming, Green, and Rich (1982) found that topics of interest included housing needs, advocacy, mental health, program development, and consumer protection, to name but a few. Churchill (1985) in a survey of nursing home and community practitioners reported interest in the physical aspects of aging, psychosocial aspects of aging, drug use, diseases of old age, nutrition, and counseling older people. Ciferri (1983) found a similar distribution of interests in a survey of nursing home personnel. Preferred topics included communicating with the elderly, death and dying, and affective needs in later life. Ciferri as well as Prothero and Kethley (1983) concluded that respondents were more interested in skills than knowledge.

One difficulty in seeking suggestions from current practitioners on appropriate educational topics is their perception that their situation and agency is unique and shares few similarities with that of others (Tobin, Davidson, and Sack 1976). Practitioners also report that the demands in their agency are so varied that no single academic background is adequate to prepare senior staff for employment there. As a result, many practitioners think that they will gain little from a group instructional program, and they seek out help from other practitioners on a one-to-one basis.

In order for continuing education to gain wide acceptance, it will be necessary to show that its impact is at least equal to its cost. Several studies have attempted to do this by examining the changes in knowledge, skills, or attitudes that result from instructional programs. In general, the findings lead to only cautious support. For example, Riddick (1985) reported that a workshop involving twenty people resulted in change in gerontological knowledge as measured by the Facts on Aging Quiz but no change in attitudes toward older people; Kethley and Pratt (1983) reported some changes in knowledge, as did Mullins and Merriam (1983).

All of these developments do not form the basis for a real program of continuing education for any individual professional. Although numerous workshop and conference opportunities exist, there are few places where an individual can find a "sequenced program" of noncredit course work that will provide comprehensive preparation for employment. Many colleges and universities offer credit courses that lead to a degree, certificate, or other credential, but there is no system for collecting and validating noncredit, occasional educational endeavors into a plan or credential. Individuals are left to identify and choose among such programs on their own initiative, which frequently leads to their having less than total understanding of aging and the service delivery system.

Conclusion and Recommendations

Continuing education of gerontology practitioners has grown rapidly but still does not approach the extent and quality needed to upgrade practice in the field successfully. Although continued growth in the number and diversity of workshops, conferences, summer courses, and seminars is appropriate, it will be necessary for some changes to be made in order that several needs currently facing the field are addressed. These needs include the very large proportion of persons who have had little or no preservice gerontology instruction, the limited degree to which current "academic gerontology" courses deal with the content most needed and wanted by practitioners, the lack of a ladder concept on which to build continuing professional education, the total absence of a national plan for gerontology continuing education, and inadequate recognition of the opportunities for continuing upgrading of even the most knowledgeable gerontology professionals.

The large number of unprepared persons currently employed in the field of aging provides the first challenge. These people need some understanding of the basics of gerontology and program operation, including the multiple processes of aging, the implications of these processes for persons in later life, and an awareness of the history and extent of the current aging services system. Many continuing education programs are aimed at this need, but these programs have not been successful in reaching a very high proportion of the appropriate persons in the field. More of these programs are needed, and the responsibility cannot be left solely to the practitioners. Employers will need to expand ways of encouraging educational upgrading through release time, tuition reimbursement, instruction provided within the agency facilities, and development of closer ties with instructional providers.

The second concern involves the relationship between practitioners and educators. When college and university gerontology faculty have been involved in offering continuing education programs, they have relied too heavily on their academic course outlines, leaving practitioners feeling that the information was irrelevant to their situations or was so abstract that it could not be applied. Instructors need to become more aware of the problems that practitioners face and to build a curriculum from that orientation. Too few college faculty are regularly involved with practitioners and do not offer information directly relevant to their interests and needs. The short-term training industry has grown up as a response to the need for more targeted instruction. However, it also causes a different problem: the lack of a cumulative credential from multiple continuing education courses.

Third, the current offerings of continuing education, both those of higher education and those of other organizations, do not lead to the acquisition of any credential that is meaningful in the field. Although certificates of completion are often awarded, they can not be applied toward the acquisition of an academic certificate or degree. Noncredit continuing education needs to be restructured so that a specified number of workshops or learning experiences can be translated into academic credit and then applied toward a college degree. This is a very thorny issue and will not be easily resolved. However, at present, a practitioner who completes many noncredit workshops gains no rewards other than the intrinsic ones of greater knowledge and self-satisfaction. The student completing a preservice program leaves the college with a credential that has the extrinsic value of being recognized widely and deserving of a higher salary in the job market. The continuing education student leaves with nothing that currently has meaning. This author's preference is that continuing education offerings be tied to academic credit, but other approaches are available, such as awarding continuing education units (CEUs) that accumulate and eventually result in a noncredit certificate. The specific mechanism is not crucial at this time. What is crucial is the need for some consideration of a system that would make explicit the expectations for practitioners in aging and indicate the attainment of these expectations through some widely recognized credential.

This suggests the fourth point, that there is no national plan for gerontology continuing education. Federal government agencies have not been willing to take the lead in this matter; neither have other professional organizations. National associations of practitioners such as the National Council on the

Aging (NCOA) and the American Society on Aging (ASA) are taking an active role and are developing a national set of instructional options for their members. The creation of a plan for upgrading and certifying practitioners would be an appropriate step in the professionalization of the field.

Finally, even those practitioners who have successfully completed preservice gerontology instructional programs have needs for skill upgrading and continuing intellectual stimulation. We can assume that this group will grow in size in the future. As Prothero and Kethley (1983) have reported, persons in this situation are demanding advanced knowledge and subjects that are specifically tailored to their employment situations. They are less interested in general issues that are peripheral to professional practice and do not want a repeat of their academic education or a restatement of the stereotypes of aging. They want to explore developing ethical issues, to understand the most recent research, to gain some perspective on federal legislation, or to learn more about developments that will professionalize their chosen field of employment.

Movement on any of these five issues is not clearly evident at this time, but the work must be done if current practitioners are to enhance the quality of services and to upgrade the field so that it will attain the rank of a full profession.

References

Churchill, L. (1985). Delineating and refining gerontology curricula at Hutchinson Community College. Mimeo.

Ciferri, W.B. (1983). Putting the Foundations Project to work. Paper presented at the annual meeting of the Gerontological Society of America, San Francisco.

Cyr, A.B., & White, K. (1982). Demand for education among long term care administrators. *Gerontology and Geriatrics Education, 2,* 261–274.

Fanslow, A.M., Andrews, M.L., Scruggs, M., & Vaughn, G.G. (1979). *The AHEA membership survey databook: 1979.* Washington, D.C.: The American Home Economics Association.

Fleming, R.E., Jr., Green, S.E., & Rich, T.A. (1982). In-service training in gerontology: A case study of statewide needs assessment. *Educational Gerontology, 8,* 63–75.

Friedsam, H.J. (In press). Education in gerontology for service: Recurrent issues in the United States. *Educational Gerontology.*

Hirschfield, I.S. (1979). An analysis of gerontology as a multidiscipline or a profession: A 1978 perspective. Unpublished doctoral dissertation, University of Southern California.

Johnson, D.P., & Kim, P.K.H. (1984). Toward professional manpower training for gerontological social work. *Gerontology and Geriatrics Education, 4,* 39–49.

Kahl, A. (1976). Special jobs for special needs: An overview. *Occupational Outlook Quarterly, 20,* 2–5.

Kethley, A.J., & Pratt, C.C. (1983). Education and consultation as a catalyst for development of mental health services for the elderly. *Gerontology and Geriatrics Education, 3,* 285–289.

Klegon, D. (1980). Education and attitudes toward training and professionalism among practitioners in the field of aging. *Educational Gerontology, 5,* 211–224.

Krishef, C.H. (1982). Who works with the elderly? A study of personnel in gerontological settings. *Educational Gerontology, 8,* 259–268.

Mullins, L.C., & Merriam, S. (1983). An experimental study of the impact of a short-term training program in death on nursing home nurses. *Gerontology and Geriatrics Education, 3,* 213–221.

National Data Base on Aging. (1986). Staffing patterns and functions of state and area agencies. Washington, D.C.: National Association of State Units on Aging and National Association of Area Agencies on Aging.

Peterson, D.A., Donahue, W.T., & Tibbitts, C. (1972). Faculty seminar in social gerontology: A model for the expansion of gerontological instruction: *Aging and Human Development, 3,* 253–260.

Prothero, J., & Kethley, A.J. (1983). Gerontologic continuing education: Do professionals seek education or training? *Gerontology and Geriatrics Education, 4,* 119–130.

Riddick, C.C. (1985). The impact of an inservice educational program on the gerontological knowledge and attitudes of geriatric recreational service providers. *Educational Gerontology, 11,* 127–135.

Simonson, W. (1981). Educational needs of the long term care pharmacy practitioner. Paper presented at the 11th annual meeting of the American Society of Consultant Pharmacists.

Strasburg, D.M. (1984). Gerontological instruction in entry-level physical therapy education. *Gerontology and Geriatrics Education, 4,* 65–73.

Tibbitts, C. (1980). Training. In H.R. Johnson (Ed.), *Academic gerontology: Dilemmas of the 1980's.* Ann Arbor: University of Michigan Institute of Gerontology.

Tobin, S.S., Davidson, S.M., & Sack, A. (1976). *Effective social services for older Americans.* Ann Arbor: University of Michigan Institute of Gerontology.

9
Future Issues in Professional Gerontology

I n order to continue developing, the professional side of the field of gerontology will need to address several issues that currently remain unresolved. These issues deal primarily with quality. They include the extent to which standards for instructional programs are developed and implemented, the licensing or certification of gerontology practitioners, and measurement of the quality of services provided by gerontological professionals.

The Need for Professional Gerontology Instruction

If this book makes a single argument, it is that gerontology can be seen as a developing profession and that to support this development, gerontology instruction needs to be organized and conducted in a way that enhances the status and performance of gerontology practitioners. As has been pointed out, this is not the only orientation of the field of gerontology, but it is the one that is rapidly growing and that currently encompasses most of the personnel who are employed in the field.

The argument, therefore, is that gerontology instruction should not be seen primarily in terms of liberal and scientific outcomes, but that it should become a more significant means of preparing people for professional roles. This does not immediately strike one as a very controversial position. Not many people will oppose preparing professionals for service to others, especially when the others are rapidly increasing in numbers and many are in need of assistance. However, most current gerontology instruction does not have this orientation.

Most gerontology instruction is built upon a model that was developed in the 1950s. It emphasizes disciplinary approaches: psychology of aging, sociology of aging, biology of aging, and perhaps policy or political science of aging. Occasionally some interdisciplinary courses replace these, but both the titles and the content retain the scientific orientation. The need is to develop course work that is based on practice skills and to make it specifically gerontological in application and purposes.

It is not readily apparent how this is to be done. The development of clear gerontological skills remains to be undertaken. Until there is more clarity in this area, gerontology instruction will consist of teaching generic human service or administrative skills that are applied to an aging setting. This application is vital. It is done through the use of examples and case studies that relate to older people and through applications in agencies that are exclusively or primarily oriented to serving the older population. Thus, students in a gerontology curriculum will gain many of the same skills as students in other professions, but in addition they will understand the way that these skills must be modified in order to be used most effectively with older people. Further, they will know how these skills best fit with the organizations and institutions that serve the elderly.

The argument, then, is not that gerontology is totally unique. The argument is that no other instructional program provides a place in which a student can select skills that are best used with older people, provides familiarity with the service agencies that relate to older people, or creates the helpful networking with the field of aging that is needed to secure and maintain employment in or related to gerontology.

Setting Standards for Gerontology Instruction

College level instruction is the principal means of preparing an individual to enter professional service. Since training programs offered at colleges and universities vary, there is a need to assume that instruction in these programs is generally equivalent so that students completing different programs will know similar content and will have comparable skills. In many professions, assurance of consistent quality is accomplished through the development and dissemination of some programmatic guidelines by a national association of instructional programs. For instance, the Council on Social Work Education has done this for the field of social work, while the American Association of Colleges of Nursing promulgates guidelines for the field of nursing. Attempts to develop instructional standards can take the form of accreditation or a less formal approach—the development of voluntary guidelines.

Accreditation of professional programs typically involves a self-study by the institution, some goal setting, development and application of some evaluation measures, and a visit by an outside team of faculty to confirm that the goals are relevant to the mission of the institution and within the parameters set by the whole profession. Accrediting frequently includes a review of such areas as: organization, administration, and governance of the institution; faculty qualification, teaching load, and student-faculty ratio; admission requirements and retention of students; curriculum content and balance; library and other facilities; and finances (Glidden 1983). Current accreditation processes no longer deal exclusively with quantitative measurements of these elements, but rather include a qualitative process that recognizes and encourages differences among programs. Accreditation relies heavily on volunteerism, self-regulation, self-evaluation, and concern for quality (Young 1983).

At the present time there is no accredition of gerontology programs per se. Although some leading faculty members have called for the development of the accreditation process (Seltzer 1985), there have been no visible attempts to achieve that end for the field of gerontology. Certain other professional associations include some form of gerontology instruction in their accreditation reviews, but no organization exists that generates a list of "approved" programs and can inform the interested student or faculty member what criteria must be met in order to achieve that designation.

The second approach to enhancement of program quality is the development and dissemination of voluntary guidelines for gerontology instruction. Establishing guidelines would first mean gathering a national group to describe the current range of gerontology instruction and develop some recommendations regarding the type and extent of curricula. These guidelines would be totally voluntary, with no sanctions imposed upon those programs that do not choose to follow them. They would allow more diversity than would accreditation and generally would not involve a visitation team. Establishing guidelines would mean an informal approach to enhancing program quality at a much lower cost than accreditation, without the need for administration by an ongoing national organization.

The development and promulgation of guidelines is a way of providing some advice to new programs or those undergoing change without resorting to the bureaucracy, regulations, and expensive processes involved in accreditation. However, guidelines would not assure the public that all programs preparing gerontologists are meeting generally agreed-upon standards in terms of the skills and knowledge of the graduates.

At present, there are no real guidelines for gerontology instruction. Two major projects have provided some suggestions: the Foundations for Gerontological Education (Johnson et al. 1980) and the WGS Guidelines (Western Gerontological Society 1978). However, these are each several years old and provide only the beginnings of a complete statement of guidelines.

Seltzer (1983) has suggested the value of a project to identify the criteria that are most important for a program to meet. Although this specific project has yet to be developed, the Association for Gerontology in Higher Education is currently conducting a survey of gerontology instruction that will result in background data on which guidelines for the field can be based. It is expected that these data will lead to a set of guidelines on curriculum, staffing, outcomes, and resources that will be of use in developing and modifying gerontology instructional programs.

Credentials for Professionals

In the search for a professional position, credentials are extremely important. They are labels that often determine the extent and type of employment opportunities open to graduates. When links between educational programs and the job market are close, credentials become a measure of a person's capabilities. Although this is not yet the situation in gerontology, current and prospective students want to know how a gerontology credential received from a college or university will affect them in the employment market. Furthermore, employers, who use credentials as judgments of the quality and potential of individual graduates, are concerned about their validity. Likewise, federal government agencies question the outcomes of career training, and the public asks for assurance that credentials have some relation to services of reputable quality.

Credentials currently fall into three categories: degrees and academic certificates, professional registration or certification, and licenses.

Degrees and Academic Certificates. These are awarded by educational institutions for successful completion of an organized program of study. They indicate that an instructional program has been completed but do not necessarily signify competence to practice a profession (Miller and Mills 1978).

The requirements for a degree or academic certificate are typically defined in terms of the duration of study, curricular content, and academic standards. The duration for degrees is reasonably uniform, involving 60–66 semester hours of credit for the associate degree, and 120–132 credit hours for the bachelor's degree. At the graduate level, however, the duration ranges from 30 to 60 credit hours for the master's degree, and the duration for professional degrees (for example, in medicine or law) and academic doctorates (Ph.D.'s) are even less consistent.

The assessment process is frequently operationalized through the offering of courses, the completion of which will result in the award of credits that can be combined in a prescribed program of study in order for the student to receive a degree or academic certificate.

The award of the degree or academic certificate means that the individual has successfully completed the program of study; it indicates that he or she has a basic knowledge of a specified content area and can be expected to deliver adequate services with substantially more consistency than those who do not hold the credential (Miller and Mills 1978).

As was discussed in chapter 6, gerontology degrees both at the bachelor's and master's level follow the general parameters used by other fields. They are generally consistent among themselves in terms of the curricula offered, but there are few data available on whether the level of skill and knowledge achieved in a gerontology instructional program is relevant to the needs of practice or result in consistent quality. These criteria remain to be developed in the AGHE project mentioned earlier.

Academic certificates are assumed to have less consistency than degrees. No surveys of certificate curricula have been done, so there is little information on which to base any assessment of their consistency or quality. However, it is known that some colleges and universities offer certificates for one-day noncredit workshops, for conference attendance, for credit courses, and for prescribed sequences of credit courses. All of these are academic certificates, but the differences among them are so great that it is nearly impossible to make any general statement about the results achieved in this type of instruction.

In the future, it will be absolutely necessary to develop greater consistency in the use of the term *certificate*. It has no meaning as long as it can refer to such different programs. This author's preference is for it to designate a series of prescribed courses and thus be measured on the same scale as degrees and other credit instruction.

Certification. Certification or registration is the process by which a professional organization or independent external agency grants recognition to an individual who has met certain predetermined qualifications. It is not required in order to practice the profession but is an indication that the individual has achieved generally accepted standards of training and practice.

Registration or certification (the two terms are used interchangeably here) is designed to promote the professional competencies of members in a voluntary association (Miller 1976). It is provided on a voluntary basis for the purpose of indicating that some practitioners have achieved a level of competence that is recognized by their peers. This level may include graduation from an accredited program, acceptable performance on qualifying examinations, and/or completion of a given amount of work experience (Henderson 1981). This process is expected to promote professionalism, to enhance the prestige of the profession, to encourage individuals to remain in the profession, to avoid governmental regulation, to protect clients from incompetent practitioners, and to encourage practitioners to remain current and to improve their performance and proficiency (Gilley 1985).

Certification typically does not involve passing legislation or requiring that government bureaucrats oversee a field. Since it is undertaken by a professional association, both those being certified and those doing the certification are peers who are seeking the best for their field. This situation has both benefits and drawbacks. Generally, government regulation is seen as restrictive, slow, and expensive. It discourages innovation and change and may not be designed to deal with unique or unusual situations. However, without government involvement, sufficient resources may not be available to develop and monitor academic standards. On the other hand, professional associations of peers may not be rigorous enough in their oversight and might award certification to persons who are incompetent. Certification, however, is seen as an alternative to licensure, and it seems to work well for many professional fields.

Today, no national certification exists for gerontologists, but certification is practiced in related professions such as social work, nursing, and occupational therapy. This means that there is relatively little control over the quality of gerontology practice. Almost anyone can call him- or herself a gerontologist and the public has no way of knowing whether that individual is adequately prepared to offer services to older individuals or their families.

Licensing. A license is legally required in order for an individual to practice certain professions—medicine, nursing, law, and so on. Licenses are typically awarded by state government agencies to persons who meet specific requirements and are issued to ensure that public health, safety, and welfare are reasonably protected (Bratton and Hildebrand 1980).

State licensure of practitioners in a variety of fields is generally undertaken to protect the public from incompetent and unprofessional practice. It involves the passage of legislation and typically is overseen by a state board appointed by the governor or by the governor's representative. Board membership is likely to consist mostly of practitioners, with a few representatives of other constituencies. A licensed profession is generally considered to have a monopoly on the provision of service in the area, and practitioners are protected from competition with the unlicensed.

Although several related professions—nursing home administration, medicine, nursing, and psychology—have licensing laws in many states, gerontology does not. No state in the United States is currently considering such legislation, and apparently it will be some time before this type of protection for the public is commonly available. However, some observers (Liebig 1983) have argued that licensing is the first logical step in enhancing quality and that its development should take precedence over accreditation and certification.

Credentialing: Advantages and Disadvantages

The term *credentialing* is used here to include degrees, certification, and licensing. Credentialing is a means of minimizing the public risk by assuring that practitioners have achieved some mastery over relevant knowledge and skill. It can provide a system for identifying persons who meet some generally agreed-upon set of standards of care and can encourage practitioners to continue updating their knowledge and skills. It can be used as a review mechanism and can involve an oversight board that is widely representative and thus reflective of the various constituencies interested in the practice.

On the other hand, credentialing is seen by others as an impediment to innovation in service delivery and in the use of staff. A variety of regulations may exist since states' laws or boards' requirements may differ from one area to the next. This may cause difficulties and restrict mobility of practitioners from one state to another. The length of a credentialing period is also a problem. With rapid change in knowledge base and practice, credentialing for life is questionable, but standards and processes for periodic review must then be created. Credentialing may prove to be costly, bureaucratic, and slow. Its development certainly involves much work, and the process of passing state legislation or gaining peer consensus is both difficult and time consuming.

Measuring the Quality of Gerontological Practice

The argument that professional gerontologists should be credentialed through degrees, certification, or licensing, must be based on evidence that professional practice with older people is enhanced by preservice instruction and on verification of some standardized knowledge and skill. To date, this information is not available. There are few data that verify the claim that practitioners who are trained in gerontology know more, work more appropriately, and are more productive in helping older people than are persons who have no such training or are trained in related professional fields.

Although gerontology faculty believe that high-quality gerontology instruction leads to high-quality practice, only anecdotal evidence of such a relationship exists. AGHE is facilitating the planning of a study on this topic, but it cannot be assumed that one investigation will conclusively show the value of gerontology instruction. A continuing process will be needed to explore the relationship of instruction to practice. This kind of study can be performed for any level of training and in many areas of the nation; the cumulative data will finally answer the question of how important gerontology preparation is to the service of older people.

Conclusion

It seems appropriate for faculty and professionals in the field of gerontology to begin exploring the options for credentialing gerontology personnel. Licensing, with its state orientation and political implications, does not seem immediately feasible, but increasing consistency in the way in which degrees and academic certificates are awarded through the promulgation of guidelines, as well as exploring means of professional certification, does seem appropriate at this time. National organizations such as the Association for Gerontology in Higher Education are exploring the development of gerontology instructional guidelines and standards. This movement may lead to greater consistency in and value of academic gerontology credentials in the future.

The AGHE's plan calls for collection of data on the extent and consistency of current gerontology instruction in community colleges, colleges, and universities; the collation of instructional curricula into some generalized program descriptions; and the generation of guidelines that could inform new program development and provide a yardstick against which existing programs could be measured. This will be a multiple-year process, but by mid-1986 it was well under way. In the future, this plan will provide a focus for activity in enhancing the quality of gerontology instruction.

On the other hand, there has been very little movement toward creation of professional certification within gerontology. Organizations such as the American Society on Aging and the National Council on the Aging have held sessions at their annual meetings in which the topic was discussed, but no real planning is yet under way. Leadership for this task has not yet appeared, and although credentialing is needed, there is currently little evidence that it will be forthcoming in the near future.

Partly, this slow development is caused by the great diversity of service roles that gerontologists fill. It is yet to be decided whether certification should deal only with direct service providers (such as counselors, case workers, and case managers) or whether it should also be available to administrators, planners, educators, evaluators, and others. There are precedents on both sides of the issue, and thus far no decision has been made. Nor has a process been developed to make that decision.

The field of professional gerontology, then, is still in the formative stages. The growth of the older population with its need for services, the relatively open access to the labor market, and the receptivity of institutions of higher education to vocationally oriented curricula have led to the expansion of gerontology instructional programs and to growth in the number of professionals who view themselves as gerontologists. However, the quality assurance aspects of a profession—accreditation, certification, and limited entry—have not yet appeared. When this will happen remains to be seen, but it is expected that the movement toward professionalization will continue and that, in the not too distant future, gerontology will take its place alongside other professions that serve the nation's people.

References

Bratton, B., & Hildebrand, M. (1980). Plain talk about professional certification. *Instruction Innovator, 25,* 22–24, 49.

Gilley, J.W. (1985). Professional certification: The procedures established, the issues addressed and the qualification criteria adopted by professional associations and societies. Unpublished doctoral dissertation, Oklahoma State University, Stillwater.

Glidden, R. (1983). Specialized accreditation. In K.E. Young, C.M. Chambers, H.R. Kells, & Associates (Eds.), *Understanding accreditation*. San Francisco: Jossey-Bass.

Henderson, A.C. (1981). The future of the health education profession: Implications for preparation and practice. *Public Health Reports, 96,* 555–559.

Johnson, H., Britton, J., Lang, C., Seltzer, M., Stanford, E., Yancik, R., Maklan, C., & Middlesworth, A. (1980). Foundations for gerontological education. *The Gerontologist, 20,* 1–61.

Liebig, P.S. (1983). Non-ivory tower strategies for significant survival of academic gerontology in the 1980s. Paper presented at the Ninth Annual Meeting of the Association for Gerontology in Higher Education, Los Angeles.

Miller, E.L. (1976). Professionalism and its impact on accreditation-type programs. Unpublished manuscript. Ann Arbor: University of Michigan.

Miller, J.W., & Mills, O. (1978). *Credentialing educational accomplishment.* Washington, D.C.: American Council on Education.

Seltzer, M.M. (1983). A proposed sociology of gerontology. *Gerontology and Geriatrics Education, 4,* 3–9.

Seltzer, M.M. (1985). Issues of accreditation of academic gerontology programs and credentialing of workers in the field of aging. *Gerontology and Geriatrics Education, 5,* 7–18.

Western Gerontological Society. (1978). Education committee develops draft standards and guidelines. *Generations,* 43–51.

Young, K.E. (1983). Prologue: The changing scope of accreditation. In K.E. Young, C.M. Chambers, H.R. Kells, & Associates (Eds.), *Understanding accreditation*. San Fransisco: Jossey-Bass.

Index

About the Author

David A. Peterson is professor and director of the Leonard Davis School of Gerontology, Andrus Gerontology Center, University of Southern California. His teaching and research interests are in educational gerontology, the application of instructional knowledge and techniques to aging. He has published extensively, including the book *Facilitating Education for Older Learners,* which received the Phillip Frandson Memorial Award for Literature from the National University Continuing Education Association. He is a past president of the Association for Gerontology in Higher Education and is currently conducting research on the extent of gerontology instruction in American institutions of higher education and personnel supply and demand in the field of gerontology.